Cuentos para niños de 6 años

Ilustraciones:
Pilar Campos

Diseño y realización:
delicado diseño/Equipo Susaeta

Corrección:
Carmen Blázquez/Equipo Susaeta

Diseño de cubierta:
José Delicado

Campezo, 13 - 28022 Madrid
Tel.: 91 3009100 - Fax: 91 3009118
Impreso y encuadernado en España
www.susaeta.com

Cuentos para niños de 6 años

susaeta

Presentación

Cuentos para niños de 6 años, pensados especialmente para ellos. Cuentos de color azul que les encantarán; con personajes humanos y animales, muchas aventuras y siempre con un fondo de ternura y enseñanza. Historias para entretener que los niños disfrutarán tanto por su lectura como por sus bonitos dibujos.

Índice

El flautista de Hamelin

Robert Browning

El flautista de Hamelin

Hamelin era una bella ciudad amurallada, regada por un río tranquilo. Cuando sus felices habitantes descansaban, les gustaba pasear por las callejuelas y la orilla del río.

La gente vivía feliz, hasta que un mal día la ciudad se vio invadida por una plaga de ratas. Las ratas de los sótanos y las alcantarillas se paseaban tranquilamente por todos los rincones de la ciudad.

Los perros y los gatos estaban asustados. Los niños no podían salir a la calle sin que les mordieran estos asquerosos animales. La comida desaparecía de las cocinas y las despensas. Era tal el ruido que hacían las ratas con sus dientes, que los habitantes de Hamelin no podían ni dormir. ¡La situación era desesperada!

El alcalde de la ciudad dijo a los concejales:

—¡Es necesario acabar con esta plaga de ratas! Hay que buscar alguna medida. Espero sus propuestas.

Pero a nadie se le ocurría ninguna.

—Excelencia, ¿y si publicamos un bando ofreciendo una recompensa a quien consiga sacar las ratas de la ciudad?

—¡Que así se haga inmediatamente!

Un buen día apareció en el ayuntamiento un hombre alto, delgado y que vestía una larga túnica. Pero lo que más llamaba la atención eran sus intensos ojos azules. El hombre misterioso se dirigió al alcalde:

—Excelencia, poseo el poder de arrastrar detrás de mí a todos los seres de este mundo. Si lo desea, yo haré desaparecer las ratas de esta ciudad. Mi nombre es... Bueno, me llaman el Flautista Mágico.

El alcalde y sus concejales vieron que llevaba una flauta de madera en la mano.

—Excelencia, mis hazañas son conocidas en el mundo entero —continuó—. He liberado a un país de una plaga de mosquitos; otro tanto hice en Bagdad con una plaga de langostas... Pero como en esta vida todo tiene un precio, os pido mil florines de oro a cambio de hacer desaparecer las ratas de la ciudad de Hamelin.

El alcalde, entusiasmado, exclamó:

—¡No sólo le daremos mil! ¡Juro que le entregaremos diez mil florines!

—¡Claro que sí! —gritaron los concejales.

El Flautista Mágico miró al alcalde y dijo:

—Cuando acabe mi trabajo, vendré a por mil florines de oro. Eso bastará.

El flautista se fue al centro de la plaza y empezó a tocar la flauta.

—¡Qué música tan extraña! —dijeron el alcalde y los concejales.

De repente, un ratoncillo corrió a los pies del flautista y se quedó mirándolo embelesado. Al poco tiempo, los bigotes de una rata asomaron tras una esquina. Luego llegó otra y otra, hasta que vinieron miles de ratas. La gente gritaba en la plaza:

—¡Mirad! ¡Salen todas!

Las gentes de Hamelin no podían creer lo que veían. De todas las calles y rincones por donde pasaba el Flautista Mágico, salían ratas que marchaban al son de la flauta.

El músico no dejaba de tocar. Cuando las reunió a todas, caminó hacia el río. Una tras otra fueron cayendo y ahogándose en el agua.

—¡Impresionante! ¡Increíble! —exclamaban las gentes de la ciudad.

Para celebrarlo, organizaron fiestas y bailes en las calles.

De repente, apareció el Flautista Mágico en la plaza. Allí estaban el alcalde y los concejales, brindando por lo bien que les había salido todo. El flautista fue hacia el grupo y, fijando la mirada en el alcalde, le dijo:

–¡Yo he cumplido mi trato y ahora le toca a usted! Vengo a por los mil florines que acordamos.

Pero el alcalde y los concejales no tenían la intención de pagar esa cantidad.

–Te estamos muy agradecidos –dijo el alcalde–, pero tendrás que conformarte con cincuenta...

—Le recuerdo que usted y sus concejales llegaron a prometerme diez mil —dijo el flautista.

El alcalde se puso rojo de vergüenza y exclamó:

—¡Bueno, hombre! Aquello era una broma.

El flautista le miró a los ojos y dijo:

—¡Un trato es un trato! Les aseguro que se arrepentirán.

El flautista se fue al centro de la plaza y empezó a tocar una música dulce y alegre que sacaba a los niños y las niñas de sus casas.

En poco tiempo, la plaza del ayuntamiento se llenó de chavales de todas las edades que bailaban al son de la flauta.

Las casas de la ciudad quedaron vacías de niños. El flautista salió de la ciudad, torció hacia la derecha y se dirigió hacia una colina cercana. Los padres, las madres, el alcalde y los concejales se quedaron aterrorizados. Tenían miedo de que el flautista se llevase para siempre a los niños.

—¡Hijos, venid! ¡Volved a casa! —gritó un padre.

—¡Volved con mamá, hijos míos! ¡No sigáis al flautista! —exclamó una madre angustiada.

Cuando el flautista y los niños llegaron a la colina, se abrió la tierra y por allí entraron todos, menos un niño cojito, que se había quedado atrás porque andaba más despacio.

—¡Ahora no podré jugar con mis amigos! —se lamentaba el muchacho llorando.

De pronto vio que algo brillaba ante él: era la siniestra flauta. El niño la llevó a sus labios y, como tenía buena memoria para la música, tocó la melodía del flautista.

En cuanto sonaron las primeras notas, la tierra se movió bajo sus pies y la colina se abrió lentamente: uno a uno aparecieron todos sus amiguitos.

El cojito, como un héroe, fue llevado al ayuntamiento y el alcalde, avergonzado por su mala acción, le entregó como premio una bolsa de mil florines. El flautista desapareció para siempre y nunca más pudieron encontrarle.

El pescadorcito Urashima

Juan Valera

El pescadorcito Urashima

Vivía hace muchísimo tiempo, en la costa del mar de Japón, un pescadorcito llamado Urashima. Era un muchacho amable y muy hábil con la caña y el anzuelo.

Cierto día salió a pescar en su barca; pero en vez de coger un pez, ¿qué crees que pescó? Pues cogió una gran tortuga, con una concha muy dura, una cara vieja, arrugada y fea, y un rabillo muy raro.

Bueno será que sepas una cosa que, sin duda, no sabes, y es que las tortugas viven mil años; al menos las tortugas japonesas.

Urashima, que lo sabía, se dijo: «Un pez me sabrá tan bien para la comida y, quizá, mejor que la tortuga. ¿Para qué he de matar a este pobre animal y privarle de que viva aún novecientos noventa y nueve años? No, no quiero ser tan cruel. Seguro estoy de que mi madre aprobará lo que hago».

Así que echó la tortuga de nuevo al mar.

Poco después sucedió que Urashima se quedó totalmente dormido en la barca. Era tiempo muy caluroso de verano, y con el sopor de la comida no pudo resistir echarse una siesta.

Apenas se durmió salió de las olas una hermosa dama, que entró en la barca y dijo:

—Yo soy la hija del dios del mar y vivo con mi padre en el Palacio del Dragón. No fue una tortuga lo que pescaste y tan generosamente pusiste en el agua en vez de matarla.

Era yo misma.

Y siguió diciendo la bella dama:

—Fui enviada por mi padre, el dios del mar, para ver si tú eras bueno o malo. Ahora, como sabemos que eres bueno, he venido para llevarte conmigo. Si quieres nos casaremos y viviremos juntos más de mil años en el Palacio del Dragón, al otro lado de los mares azules.

Tomaron entonces Urashima un remo y la princesa otro, y remaron hasta llegar al Palacio del Dragón.

Allí vivía el dios del mar e imperaba, como rey, sobre todos los dragones, tortugas y peces.

¡Oh, qué sitio tan hermoso era aquél! Los muros del palacio eran de coral; los árboles tenían esmeraldas por hojas y rubíes por frutas; las escamas de los peces eran de plata y las colas de los dragones, de oro.

Piensa en todo lo más bonito que hayas visto en tu vida, ponlo junto y tal vez imaginarás entonces lo que aquel fabuloso palacio parecía.

Todo aquello pasó a pertenecer a Urashima por haberse convertido en yerno del dios del mar y marido de la adorable princesa.

Allí vivieron dichosos más de tres años, paseando todos los días entre aquellos árboles con hojas de esmeralda y frutas de rubí. Pero una mañana, Urashima habló con su mujer.

—Muy contento y satisfecho estoy aquí, pero necesito volver a mi casa y ver a mis padres y hermanos. Déjame ir un tiempo y volveré.

—No me gusta que te vayas —contestó ella—. Mucho temo que te suceda algo terrible. Pero vete, pues así lo deseas y no se puede evitar. Toma, sin embargo, esta caja y cuida mucho de no abrirla. Esto es lo más importante, recuérdalo, pues si la abres, no volverás a verme.

Prometió Urashima tener mucho cuidado con la caja y no abrirla por nada del mundo. Se despidió de su esposa con un dulce beso y un fuerte abrazo. Luego entró en la barca, navegó bastante tiempo por el ancho mar y, al fin, divisó tierra a lo lejos y desembarcó en la costa de su país.

Pero, ¿qué había ocurrido durante su ausencia? ¿Dónde estaba la choza de sus padres? ¿Qué había sido de la aldea en que vivía? Las verdes montañas estaban allí, como antes, muy cerca del mar, pero los árboles habían sido cortados.

El arroyuelo que corría junto a la choza de sus padres seguía corriendo, pero ya no iban allí las mujeres a lavar la ropa, como antes.

Pasó entonces un hombre con su caña de pescar por allí cerca, y el joven Urashima le preguntó:

—¿Puedes decirme, por favor, dónde está la choza de Urashima, que se hallaba aquí antes?

—¿Urashima? ¿Cómo preguntas por él, si hace cuatrocientos años que desapareció pescando? Su padre, su madre, sus hermanos, los nietos de sus hermanos, hace siglos que murieron. Ésa es una historia muy antigua. Loco debes de estar cuando buscas aún tal choza. Hace centenares de años era ya escombros.

De súbito acudió a la mente de Urashima la idea de que el Palacio del Dragón, con sus muros de coral y sus fuentes de rubíes y sus dragones con cola de oro, había de ser parte del país de las hadas, donde un día es más largo que un año en este mundo, y que sus tres años en compañía de la princesa habían sido cuatrocientos. De nada valía, pues, permanecer ya en tierra, donde todos los parientes y amigos habían muerto, y donde hasta su propia aldea había desaparecido.

Con gran precipitación y atolondramiento pensó Urashima en volver con su mujer. Pero, ¿cuál era el rumbo que debía seguir? ¿Quién se lo diría?

—Tal vez —caviló— si abro la caja que ella me dio, descubra el secreto del camino que busco.

Así desobedeció las órdenes que le había dado la princesa, o bien no las recordó en aquel momento por lo trastornado que estaba. Como quiera que fuese, Urashima abrió la caja. ¿Y qué crees que salió de allí? Salió una nube blanca que se fue flotando sobre el mar.

Gritaba él en balde a la nube que se parase. Entonces recordó con tristeza lo que su mujer le había dicho de que tras abrir la caja no habría medio de que volviese él al palacio del dios del mar. Pronto ya no pudo Urashima gritar ni correr hacia la playa en pos de la nube.

De repente, sus cabellos se volvieron blancos como la nieve, su rostro se cubrió de arrugas y su espalda se encorvó como la de un viejo. Después le faltó el aliento. Y, finalmente, cayó muerto en la playa.

¡Pobre Urashima! Si hubiera hecho lo que le dijo la princesa del Palacio del Dragón, habría vivido aún más de mil años.

La reina de las abejas

Hans Christian Andersen

La reina de las abejas

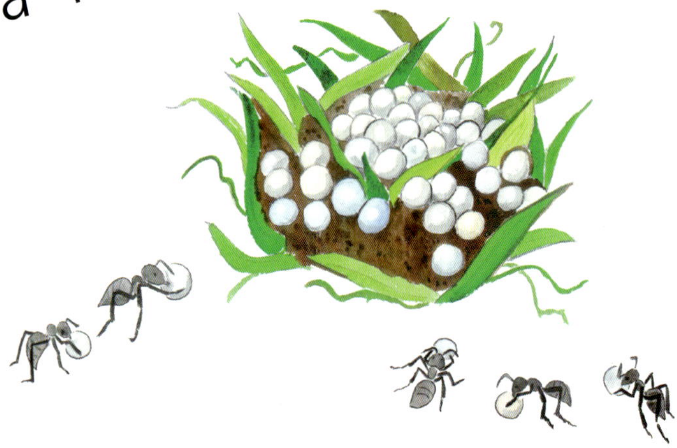

Érase una vez un rey que tenía tres hijos. Los dos mayores, que eran muy aventureros, se marcharon de palacio con la intención de conocer el mundo. Y tanto les gustó esa vida, que decidieron no volver jamás a su reino.

Como los hermanos mayores no regresaban, el más pequeño, a quien todos llamaban Bobalicón, decidió ir a buscarlos.

Cuando
por fin los encontró, sus hermanos
le dijeron:

–Vente con nosotros. Te aseguramos que te vas a divertir mucho más que en el palacio.

Y Bobalicón aceptó.

Iban los tres anda que te andarás y se encontraron con un hormiguero. Los dos hermanos mayores quisieron pisotearlo para ver cómo huían las hormigas. Pero Bobalicón no permitió que lo hicieran y les dijo:

—Pobrecitas, no las matéis; ellas también tienen derecho a vivir.

Un poco más adelante se encontraron con unos patos que nadaban en un lago. Los dos mayores quisieron coger un par de ellos para asarlos y comérselos. Pero Bobalicón no se lo permitió y les dijo:

—Pobres patos, no los matéis; ellos también tienen derecho a vivir.

Y andando andando, llegaron a un bosque. Como estaban muy cansados, los tres hermanos se sentaron debajo de un árbol en el que había una colmena de abejas.

El príncipe mayor dijo a sus hermanos:

–Mirad cómo corre la miel por el tronco del árbol. Si le prendemos fuego, las abejas se asfixiarán y podremos llevarnos la miel.

Pero Bobalicón no se lo permitió y les dijo:

–Pobres abejas, no las matéis; ellas también tienen derecho a vivir.

Siguieron caminando y llegaron a un castillo misterioso: las cuadras estaban llenas de caballos, pero no encontraron a una sola persona por ninguna parte.

Recorrieron todas las habitaciones y los salones y, al final de un pasillo, tropezaron con una puerta cerrada con tres cerrojos. En el centro había un ventanuco abierto por el que se podía mirar hacia dentro.

Los tres príncipes miraron y vieron a un hombrecillo gris sentado a una mesa repleta de deliciosos alimentos. Le llamaron una y otra vez, pero el hombrecillo parecía no oírles.

Finalmente, se levantó, les abrió la puerta y les llevó hasta la mesa para que comieran con él. Cuando se hartaron de comer y beber, el hombrecillo llevó a cada hermano a una habitación para que descansaran.

Al día siguiente, el hombrecillo gris llamó al hermano mayor y le enseñó una tablilla de piedra donde estaban escritas las tres pruebas que había que superar para desencantar el castillo. Después, le leyó la primera prueba.

—Entre la hierba del bosque están esparcidas las mil perlas de las princesas. Es necesario recogerlas todas antes de que el sol se oculte. Si faltase alguna, el muchacho que las busca se convertirá en estatua de piedra.

Entusiasmado, el hermano mayor fue al bosque. Aunque no descansó ni un segundo, sólo encontró cien perlas. Así que, cuando el sol se ocultó, quedó convertido en estatua de piedra.

Al día siguiente, el segundo hermano realizó la misma prueba y corrió la misma suerte.

Finalmente, le llegó el turno a Bobalicón. Buscó y rebuscó entre la hierba del bosque y, como apenas encontraba perlas, se puso a llorar.

Entonces, apareció la reina de las hormigas y le dijo:

—No llores más. Por haber sido tan bueno con nosotras, mis cinco mil hormigas recogerán todas las perlas.

Cuando el hombrecillo gris recibió el montón de perlas, le leyó a Bobalicón la segunda prueba.

—En el fondo del lago está la llave de la habitación de la princesa. Tráemela.

Bobalicón fue al lago y, como no sabía nadar, se puso a llorar en la orilla. Los patos a los que había salvado le dijeron:

—Nosotros, que te debemos la vida, buscaremos la llave en el fondo del lago.

Inmediatamente, los patos volvieron con la llave en el pico. Bobalicón se la llevó al hombrecillo gris y éste le leyó la tercera prueba:

—El rey tiene tres hijas que están dormidas. Averigua cuál es la más joven y la más guapa. Lo sabrás por la golosina que tomaron antes de que las venciese el sueño. La mayor comió

un terrón de azúcar; la mediana, un caramelo y la más joven tomó miel.

Aunque aquélla era la prueba más difícil, en su auxilio vino la reina de las abejas.

Probó los labios de las tres princesas y le indicó quién era la que había comido la miel.

En cuanto el príncipe señaló a la princesa más joven y guapa, el castillo quedó desencantado. Y así fue como el joven príncipe se casó con la princesa más bonita. Sus hermanos, que recobraron la forma humana, se casaron con las otras dos princesas. Y todos fueron felices y comieron perdices.

El rey Pico de Tordo

Hermanos Grimm

El rey Pico de Tordo

Éste era un rey que tenía una hija muy hermosa pero, tan orgullosa, que despreciaba a todos sus pretendientes. Para remediar aquella situación, su padre dio una gran fiesta en la que reunió a todos los hombres del reino que quisieran casarse con su hija. Los colocó en fila y la princesa los fue mirando uno a uno.

—Éste es más pequeño que un comino —dijo del primero.

—¡Qué gordo está éste! —comentó de otro.

—¡Ja, éste tiene la barbilla como el pico de un tordo!

Desde ese momento, aquel pretendiente se quedó con el mote de Pico de Tordo. El anciano rey, harto de las burlas de su hija, gritó en medio de la fiesta:

—¡Juro ante todos vosotros que la princesa se ha de casar con el primer harapiento que llame a mi puerta!

Días más tarde, un músico pobre y andrajoso se puso a cantar debajo del balcón del salón real. Cuando el soberano lo oyó, pidió a sus criados que le hicieran subir. En cuanto estuvo ante su presencia, el rey le dijo:

—Me ha gustado tanto tu voz que, en vez de unas monedas, te voy a dar la mano de mi hija.

Después, llamó a la princesa y le habló de esta manera:

—He dado mi palabra de que te casaría con el primer harapiento que llegase a palacio. Por tanto, hija mía, aquí tienes a tu marido.

—¡Pero padre...! —exclamó la joven.

Pocos minutos después, el sacerdote de palacio casaba a la princesa con el músico. Tras la ceremonia, el rey dijo a su hija:

—Como un harapiento no puede vivir bajo mi techo, te ordeno que abandones el palacio con tu esposo.

El músico, tan contento, tomó la mano de su esposa y la sacó de allí. Llevaban andando un buen rato, cuando entraron en la capital de un nuevo reino que estaba rodeada de bosque.

—¿De quién son esta ciudad y ese bosque tan enorme? —preguntó ella.

—Del rey Pico de Tordo, que quiso ser tu esposo —contestó él.

—¡
—exc
Ho
—¿
la esp
—E
—con
En
las ta
—M
Despu
La
músic
cocina

COLLECTOR'S EDITION

Entertainment WEEKLY

THE ULTIMATE GUIDE TO The Walking Dead

PHOTOGRAPH BY DYLAN COULTER

Pictured: Lauren Cohan, Andrew Lincoln, Steven Yeun and Norman Reedus

CONTENTS

THE TWO COVERS
This collector's edition of *Entertainment Weekly* has two front covers, one of the living, one of the undead.

INSIDE: ORIGINAL ART!
All the season chapters open with panels that trace the journey of survivors in the series, created by the artists who draw *The Walking Dead* comic books.

PHOTOGRAPH BY DYLAN COULTER

Undeath Becomes Him

I've watched the series go from cult hit to cultural movement, and served as fan ambassador, zombie therapist and full-time *Walking Dead* Customer Service Desk. What keeps me glued to the screen? The stories, the cast and crew, sure—but most of all, the community.

BY CHRIS HARDWICK

THE FIRST TIME I SAW *THE WALKING Dead* was at San Diego Comic-Con, 2010. I was there with a few friends, and we wandered by the AMC booth on the convention floor, where they were playing the trailer for this wild new adaptation of the comic. The trailer played, and all of us reflexively uttered strings of excited expletives—which I'm not allowed to write here because people are sensitive about swearing but fine watching a show where people's brains get stabbed out of their heads.

We watched the trailer play five more times. When I got back to L.A., I was able to obtain the press screener, which was only the first two episodes. I was hooked. Immediately. "'Cuz if there really was a zombie apocalypse," I'd prattle on to whoever wouldn't walk away from me, *"that's what it would actually be like."* Having to wait for the remaining episodes to air was like being in a middle seat and having to pee—I needed relief. When I finally got it, *TWD* became my new favorite show.

Early the next year I caught wind that AMC might experiment with an aftershow that would wrap up all the action. It was a naive time before rhymes were fully understood, so it was referred to simply as *The Walking Dead Aftershow*. At the same time I was pursuing the job, I got a call from one of the executives at AMC who just happened to have been my first television boss when I worked at MTV back in the 1900s. It's a good lesson, kids! Never give up and you too can have the kind of career that keeps coming back from the dead.

And thus began one of the most significant journeys of my life. In the last five years I've gotten to be the weird Cousin Oliver peering in through the window of *The Walking Dead*—the overexcited towheaded boy who is *sort of* involved with the show and stands proudly near it. The show is beautifully shot and directed, with stunning special effects (no one else was skilled enough to do good zombies on high-def TV before Greg Nicotero), masterfully written and brilliantly acted (Emmys: *Nominate these people*), and yet those things only account for a hit show. What makes it a monster-hit-global-phenomenon-pop-culture-defining monolith is one simple word—community. It's an "Inception" of community layers: *The Walking Dead* is a show about a tight community made by a tight community for a tight community. It makes us face the most basic questions about who we'd become in an extreme world and who would be there with us.

The people who make the show are genuinely some of the most wonderful people, who care deeply about each other and understand that this experience is the most rarefied of TV air. They are not just actors taking a paycheck for a job, they are also a *part* of the fan community. You can feel it when you view their Instagrams or see any pics pop up on the Internet with excited Walking Deadheads who spotted them in the wild. They happily take the time to share in that excitement with those who have made it a part of their lives.

I've never seen a show that had a following with such a broad age range—kids, parents, grandparents. This show is a bonding ritual for them. I've been lucky enough to meet thousands of them, from little girls who've told me they want to be Michonne to grandpas who tell me how to recycle poop to grow crops if society falls. (Well, one guy. True story.) We are part of a worldwide club that can immediately connect on who might die next in the show, what our zombie apocalypse escape plan is, which Abraham Ford-ism best describes us (me: dolphin smooth) and, of course, CORALLLLLLL.

From the bottom of my edible heart I would like to very sincerely thank both *The Walking Dead*'s team for adopting me and the legion of amazing fans for allowing me to be an annoyingly enthusiastic part of your Sunday-night ritual.

"WE ARE PART OF A WORLDWIDE CLUB THAT CAN IMMEDIATELY CONNECT ON . . . WHAT OUR ZOMBIE APOCALYPSE PLAN IS"

—CHRIS HARDWICK

EVERYTHING IN MODERATION
Left: Chris Hardwick during his live aftershow. Top, from left to right: creator Robert Kirkman, showrunner Scott M. Gimple, Jeffrey Dean Morgan, Norman Reedus and Hardwick on *Talking Dead*. Middle: Hardwick and the cast clown around during their Comic-Con panel. Bottom: Hardwick meets a few avid Deadheads.

Why We Love Zombies

Ever since they shambled onscreen with *White Zombie* and feasted on flesh in *Night of the Living Dead*, the undead have managed to bring our imaginations to vivid life again and again. —JEFF JENSEN

LONG BEFORE ZOMBIES ruled the school, they were the drooling losers of Monster High. Shuffling and mindless and dreadfully grungy in their fashion sense, zombies lacked the romantic suck of vampires, the tortured mooniness of werewolves, the cosmic horror of predatory extra-terrestrials or the gotcha mischief of poltergeists. But quietly (or at least with a hungry, monotone grumble), and with a patient persistence that only an unstoppable eating machine can muster, zombies have shambled into their prime. AMC's *The Walking Dead* is the peak expression of a slow-moving outbreak that has transformed cinematic storytelling and seized the zeitgeist of an anxious nation fixated on apocalypse of all sorts—political, social, economic, technological, spiritual. We can't stop looking at them, and being scared by them, because they reflect back the subject that fascinates us and terrifies us the most: ourselves.

In truth, zombies have been malingering, waiting for their moment since the Big Bang of big-screen horror: Universal's monster movies of the early '30s. Those early beasts weren't yet the plague-infected people-eaters of modern times. Bela Lugosi, newly fanged with superstardom thanks to *Dracula*, launched the subgenre with *White Zombie* (1932), playing the lead, a western witch doctor. *White Zombie*'s legacy includes "cult film" veneration and rocker-turned-horror auteur Rob Zombie's band of the same name.

But the zombie genre as we know it today crawled to life via the phenomenon of George A. Romero's *Night of the Living Dead* (1968) and its sequels. Loosely inspired by the plague-infected vampiric mutants of Richard Matheson's 1954 last-man-on-earth novel *I Am Legend* (an influence on much post-WWII horror), Romero gave zombies a makeover inside and out. They became mysteriously reanimated cannibal corpses—a new gloss on the ancient ghoul archetype—and symbols for consumerism, racism, conformism, all sorts of "-isms" of late-'60s society, turning the zombie movie into subversive allegory. As an ingeniously shot DIY cheapie, *Night of the Living Dead* helped launch a new generation of counterculture independent filmmaking. As a taboo-smashing fangoria, the film fueled another emerging genre: splatter horror. Both distinctions would inspire a host of future filmmakers, including John Carpenter and Sam Raimi. All zombie pop since Romero, including *The Walking Dead*, is either homage or response to his groundbreaking work.

And yet zombies remained a Romero cottage industry or the stuff of low-budget grind-house schlock for decades. Until the 1990s, perhaps the most iconic moment in zombie pop was… Michael Jackson's "Thriller" video. Line-dancing ghouls are hard to take seriously, even with Vincent Price's menacing rap narration. The metamorphosis toward respectability and ubiquity began when video games sank their teeth into zombies; made them a staple in their visceral, viscera-splashy horror/sci-fi shooters; and turned them into antagonists worthy of a challenge—faster, raging, massive in number, unrelenting. They seeded the imagination of a whole new generation of pop consumers and filmmakers. *Resident Evil* (1996), a game changer, became not only a blockbuster movie franchise but inspired the two other films credited with catalyzing the new-century zombie-pop boom: *28 Days Later* (2003), directed by Danny Boyle, and the clever, romantic pop pastiche *Shaun of the Dead* (2004), helmed by Edgar Wright. Combined with Zack Snyder's remake of *Dawn of the Dead* (2004), these films—made with fanboy passion, plus a polish and panache

THE INFECTION SPREADS Max Brooks's bestselling apocalyptic horror novel *World War Z* hit the big screen in 2013, starring Brad Pitt (top).

SOMETHING EVIL'S LURKING Jackson's 1983 "Thriller" (far left) inspired a Guinness World Record group dance, with 13,597 participants. Duane Jones and Judith O'Dea in Romero's *Night of the Living Dead* (middle). Low-budget horror film *Teenage Zombies* featured a crazed scientist (left).

unusual for the genre—spurred a sea change. Zombies were no longer camp, they were cool. An audience jittery about terrorism, recession, the environment and more helped the shift—and with it came a boom of apocalyptic survival fantasy.

It was at this moment that Robert Kirkman pitched Image Comics on a zombie series inspired by the thing he liked least about zombie movies: that they had to end. He envisioned a gritty and gory existential saga that started where most zombie outbreak finished, with the despairing realization that there was no cure and life was now a never-ending struggle to avoid infection and survive. The publisher blanched. "There had never been a successful zombie book in the history of comics," Kirkman explained in the 2014 documentary *The Image Revolution*. Kirkman turned their lukewarm interest into an enthusiastic one by promising a sci-fi twist: The zombie onslaught would be explained as the prelude to an alien invasion. After the third issue Kirkman came clean. He never had any intention of following through on the gambit. "I kind of tricked them into accepting *The Walking Dead*."

TWD should have been a no-brainer for new-century television. It played to three superpopular trends: fantastical cliffhanger serials like *Lost*, soul-scuzzing antihero wallows like *Breaking Bad* and comic-booky everything. But it earned worthy points for innovation too. Its production values and visceral storytelling raised the game for television, from the exquisitely repellent artistry of makeup master Greg Nicotero to the fight-or-flight action sequences that were brilliant in their direction, cinematography and sound design. Yes, it revels in sensationalism, as zombie spectacle is wont to do. The episode "Guts," in which the show's hero-in-chief, former lawman Rick Grimes (a superb, underrated Andrew Lincoln), leads his cohorts in dressing in the entrails of the newly dead to throw zombies off their scent, is a gross-out masterpiece.

Yet *The Walking Dead*'s most meaningful contribution to the genre has been its ambition to move (and frighten) us with the desperate flail of its survivor-heroes to remain human, spiritually more than physically, amid despairing and degrading circumstances. Watching the likes of Rick and Carol (Melissa McBride) gradually traverse the slippery slope from idealistic law-keepers to realpolitik nihilists—and, conversely, watching ragged lone-wolf Daryl (Norman Reedus) slowly find more meaning in community and selflessness—has often made for surprisingly deep soap. It owes a deep debt to its original showrunner, Frank Darabont (*The Shawshank Redemption*, *The Mist*), a filmmaker skilled at blending modern and old-school horror and finding poignancy in the pulp. Darabont minted a recurring motif intrinsic to the meaning of the show: framing moments of profound suffering with overhead shots, a heavenly view of human misery implicit with yearning for angelic intervention and complaint about divine distance. *The Walking Dead* isn't as heady or cunning in its allegory of materialism, society and man's inhumanity to man as Romero's films, but it does pulse with the fret of post-9/11 America, the fear that we've become monstrous in our response to tragedy, wondering if our dysfunction is beyond repair.

Entering its seventh season, *The Walking Dead* remains popular at a time media is crowded with zombie allegorica, from the White Walkers (and Jon Snow) of HBO's *Game of Thrones* to undead detective Olivia "Liv" Moore in The CW's *iZombie* (which, like *TWD*, originated as a comic). Both shows represent something new to the genre: a glimmer of hope. The White Walkers could represent a cynical judgment against a fallen world—or an opportunity for fractured people to come together and fight for their common welfare and new meaning. Liv Moore is a more dynamic metaphor. Yeah, she can go "full zombie mode" berserk when attacked, stressed or starved. (Don't we all?) But feasting exclusively on the brains of murder victims and gaining their memories and personas, Liv becomes an agent for justice and grows in empathy. These next-gen revenant tales round out the portrait of our times. In the words of Rick Grimes, we are the walking dead. But as stories of zombie apocalypse rage on, they may show us the way to rehumanization.

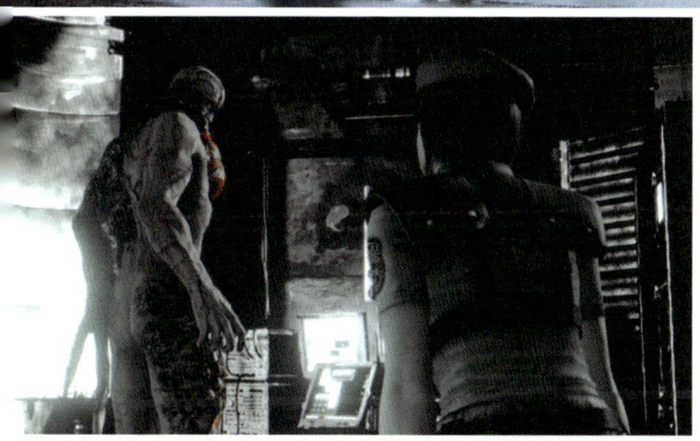

“THE ORIGINAL *NIGHT OF THE LIVING DEAD* IS OUR BOOK OF GENESIS”

—FRANK DARABONT

FEAR FACTORS
Clockwise from top: Danny Boyle's *28 Days Later*; the video game that inspired the blockbuster movie *Resident Evil*; literary mash-up *Pride and Prejudice and Zombies*; George Romero's 1979 *Dawn of the Dead*; CW's *iZombie*, adapted from the comic of the same name by Chris Roberson and Michael Allred; Simon Pegg's loving parody *Shaun of the Dead*.

Bat Out of Hell

Fans may be agonizing over *TWD*'s big cliff-hanger, but they really should be more concerned about what happens in the rest of season 7—it's Negan's world now

THERE'S A NEW BOSS IN ALEXANDRIA. NEGAN HAS arrived, and he's brought his army of Saviors—along with a barbed-wire-covered baseball bat affectionately referred to as Lucille—with him.

On this steamy June day of filming on the Senoia, Ga., set, Negan visits the pantry to check out the ammunition supply. Then Jeffrey Dean Morgan, who has been tasked with bringing the ultimate comic-book villain to life, lets it fly. "Are you getting f---ing uppity on me?" he asks an Alexandrian. Apparently, Morgan enjoys sprinkling in some of the saltier language that made the character so infamous in comic form.

The thing about Morgan's F-bombs is that you never quite know when and where they are going to detonate. None of these profanity-laced ad-libs are in the script, and none will actually make it to air. "We push it as far as what I can and can't say," Morgan explains a week later while in New York City. "I memorize it two ways: I learn what's okay for TV, and then I learn the Negan way, which is nothing barred. . . . And I will add

Jeffrey Dean Morgan photographed for *Entertainment Weekly* in Atlanta on July 9, 2016.

PHOTOGRAPH BY MATTHIAS CLAMER

every "f---," "f---ing," "f---ety f---" and more, just to f---ing get a reaction."

Getting a reaction is what *TWD* has been specializing in lately. Fans went ballistic when season 6 of the AMC drama ended with Negan taking batting practice on an unknown someone's face. Executive producers Scott M. Gimple, Robert Kirkman and Greg Nicotero all admit to being surprised by the intensity of the anger. They are also careful to respect those opinions while defending their work.

The wait for answers has proved difficult for many. Norman Reedus (Daryl Dixon) estimates he is asked "30 times a day" to reveal the identity of the deceased. Andrew Lincoln (Rick Grimes) says he has been interrogated while going through customs. Lennie James (Morgan) jokes that his solution to avoid the topic is that he has simply "stopped speaking to people." And then there is Melissa McBride (Carol), who has to deal with her own mother. "She's like, 'I want to know who died,'" says McBride. "And then I was talking to her just days ago, and she was like, 'Did you die?' I'm like, 'Mom, I wasn't *in* that scene!'"

Season 7 will be a pretty brutal experience right off the bat—no pun intended. "I can tell you from the position of the director's chair, it was by far the most emotional episode that I've ever shot," says Nicotero of the season premiere.

The cast had to enter a dark place to film the continuation to the cliff-hanger scene. "It was exhausting, and it was no fun," says Reedus. "We always come back to this show every season, and we're like, 'Yeah, let's get back into it!' This was one of those where it's like, 'Oh f---. Here we go.' It was definitely not a joyous reunion."

While there have been plenty of big offings before, Lincoln says this one "is the most significant death that we've ever experienced in the show for what it does to the story." Indeed, how will each individual react to a murder they were powerless to prevent—one that happened as they sat next to the victim? "It affects the group completely differently," says Reedus. "Some relinquish power. Some accept it. . . . Some fight it. The group is completely broken apart at this point."

▲ **HOLDING OUT HOPE** Lennie James's Morgan must face his season 6 decision to abandon his no-killing policy. "The important thing to remember about Morgan is that it's not just that he doesn't want to kill people," says James. "It's that he knows what he's like when he's free to kill people. He knows himself. He's good at it and he's pathological at it, and it's not a road he particularly wants to walk down."

◀ **WILD KINGDOM** New cast member Khary Payton runs the Kingdom as Ezekiel (far left). Jeffrey Dean Morgan promises audiences will quickly "find out how Negan has come to be who he is" (left).

That's because they are no longer in charge and they're no longer the biggest badasses around. Or, as Jeffrey Dean Morgan so eloquently states, "It's f---ing Negan's world now."

What does all this mean for the Alexandrians? "Some of your characters that you've grown to love are not going to be on the show anymore, and it's going to end badly for them," Morgan says. "You're going to see your favorite characters in a position that they've never been in before, which is super-vulnerable and victimized."

Negan's compound the Sanctuary (which Gimple calls "a pretty epic location") is not the only new site in season 7. Carol and Morgan were last seen in the company of some armored soldiers offering assistance from a community known as the Kingdom and its equal parts kooky and charismatic leader King Ezekiel, played by Khary Payton. It won't take long for Carol and Morgan to realize they aren't exactly in Kansas anymore. "It's the *Walking Dead* version of *The Wizard of Oz*," says Nicotero of the Kingdom. "If the outside is a black-and-white dull, dead world, the inside is vibrant and colorful and whimsical and alive, and it's all led by a dude named Ezekiel with a scepter and a f---ing tiger. At first glance you look at this and you go, 'This can't be real.'"

"You first come upon him and you think he's a little bit out-there," says Payton. Comic-book creator Kirkman admits, "That's probably the wildest swing I took in the comics. A guy who has a pet tiger who speaks like some kind of weird medieval king is pretty strange." Ezekiel's tiger, whom he calls Shiva, is brought to life through a mix of animatronics and digital augmentation.

At least Carol and Morgan are, you know, alive. The same cannot be said for at least one individual from Negan's lineup. And while some fans may bemoan the six-month wait to find out who is destined to die, the man swinging the bat has a warning for all those pining for answers. Morgan channels his inner Negan while breaking out that disarming, devilish grin. "You have to be careful what you wish for, audience, because you're going to get those answers and more. And you're probably not going to be happy with it." —DALTON ROSS

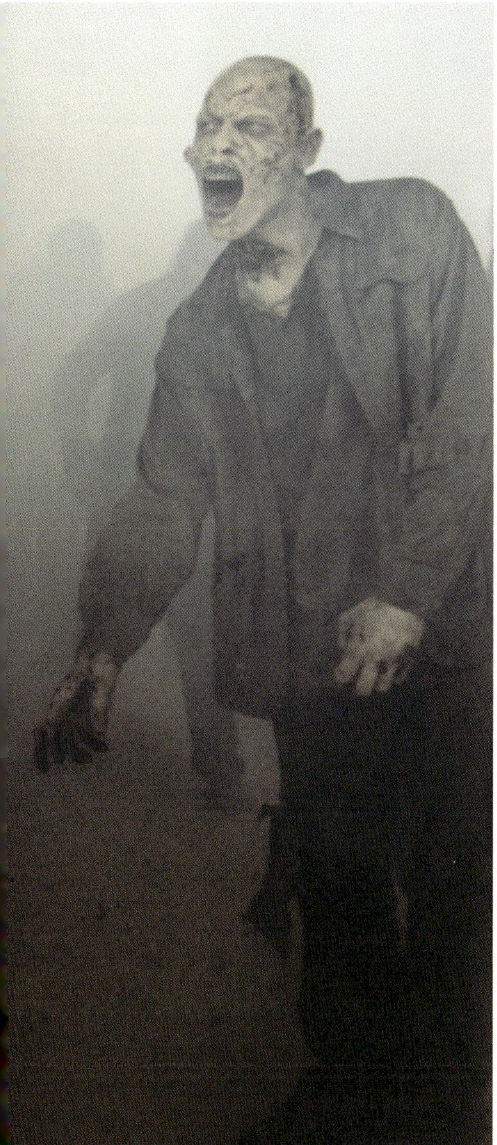

▲

UNDEAD AND LOVING IT The tiger may be partially computer-generated, but the zombies are real, created under the supervision of makeup SFX whiz Greg Nicotero.

◀

LOAVES AND FISHES Tom Payne returns as Paul "Jesus" Rovia, who proved himself a friend to the Alexandrians by arranging for food and supplies to be delivered from the Hilltop (far left). Melissa McBride seeks shelter as Carol, who is safe from Negan—at least for now (left).

LETHAL WEAPON

SPEAK LOUDLY & CARRY LUCILLE

Here's Negan, the prequel series to *The Walking Dead*, is filled with revelations about the foul-mouthed villain, including the fact that his bat was named after his late wife. So who meets Lucille, then meets his/her maker in the season 6 finale?

Potential victims include a who's who of primary characters, including Glenn (have you *read* the comic books?); Abraham (karma for dumping Rosita, perhaps); Maggie (a grim twofer, as she's pregnant with Glenn's baby); Michonne (because Rick's love interests always die); and Sasha (it would be a warrior's death).

SEASON 1

SHIT.

After the World Dies

It began with a cop in a cowboy hat. Alone on a desolate roadside strewn with abandoned cars and grisly corpses, Rick Grimes searches for signs of life

WHEN *THE WALKING DEAD* ARRIVED IN THE fall of 2010, it was like nothing else on TV: serialized, splatter-shock horror. Critics took notice, lavishing praise on the show's thrilling urgency and stunning visuals. The series soon earned record ratings for cable TV as millions of viewers tuned in to follow Rick Grimes and his fellow survivors struggle to navigate a postapocalyptic state of Georgia, overrun by "walkers," as the undead are called here.

All of that was pretty impressive for a show that almost didn't happen. After falling in love with Robert Kirkman's acclaimed comic book series, Frank Darabont (director of *The Green Mile* and *The Shawshank Redemption*) started pitching his vision for a TV adaptation back in 2005. No one bit. Network rejections piled up, and for years his pilot script seemed doomed—until producer Gale Anne Hurd brought the show to AMC's attention. The cable network had recently rebranded itself

DEATH AND AXES Their jackets splattered with gore in an attempt to conceal their scent, Rick (Andrew Lincoln) aggressively confronts a walker as Glenn (Steven Yeun) looks on. Comic pages from *The Walking Dead* No. 2; art by Tony Moore (previous spread).

with scripted titles such as *Mad Men* and *Breaking Bad*. A series like *The Walking Dead* presented another, even splashier opportunity to branch out.

In early 2010 the cable network bought an entire season on the spot, with one hitch: They wanted to debut the series by Halloween, which put Darabont under extreme pressure. "It was literally like surviving a zombie apocalypse," he said of the time crunch. "There weren't zombies trying to eat us, but the schedule certainly was." His team, which included Kirkman and make-up-effects wizard Greg Nicotero, spent the following summer in Atlanta madly rushing to write, cast and shoot a story arc that could establish *The Walking Dead*'s unique world, its core characters, and their complex relationships—all in just six episodes.

Remarkably it worked. Set in a vividly realized world full of flesh-eating walkers, the series centered on a ragtag band of survivors: Rick Grimes, a former sheriff's deputy who becomes the show's de facto leader (played by Andrew Lincoln, a theater-trained Brit best known at the time for *Love Actually*); his strong-willed wife, Lori (Sarah Wayne Callies, who had small roles in network procedurals); his young son Carl (a then 10-year-old Chandler Riggs); and Rick's supposed best friend, the hotheaded Shane (stage and TV vet Jon Bernthal). Joining them were crafty delivery boy Glenn (Korean-born Steven Yeun, who performed improv at the Second City), redneck brothers Daryl and Merle (motorcycle enthusiast/action-movie staple Norman Reedus and dramatic actor Michael Rooker), meek domestic-abuse victim Carol (Melissa McBride, with a résumé filled with made-for-TV movies), hard-nosed lawyer Andrea (Laurie Holden, with a history of genre television) and other everyday citizens just trying to stay alive. "This is about a group of people who are forced to survive together, be a family together and endure very, very difficult circumstances," says Darabont.

The short season culminated with the gang storming the CDC headquarters in a desperate bid to find answers. Instead they found a lone, suicidal doctor. Not willing to give up, Rick and his followers left to embark on their next journey, one of many to come. —RAY RAHMAN

WAKING NIGHTMARE
Front row, from left to right: Lori Grimes (Sarah Wayne Callies), Carl Grimes (Chandler Riggs), Andrea's sister Amy (Emma Bell), Dale (Jeffrey DeMunn) and Shane (Jon Bernthal). The survivors pick up a distressing radio call from their hilltop refuge outside of Atlanta (top left). Meanwhile, a bewildered Rick Grimes wanders through his abandoned hospital after he rises from his coma (top right).

PLAN OF ATTACK
Merle Dixon (Michael Rooker) gets physical with T-Dog (IronE Singleton) on the roof of a department store (far left). Extras dressed as walkers swarm a fence (middle). During a break in shooting, Lincoln and steed take a break from battling the undead (left).

DEAD MAN WALKING Rick watches where he steps after rising from his hospital bed to discover civilization has imploded due to a zombie pandemic (above).

CAPTURING THE MOMENT Frank Darabont sets the scene with a walker while directing the pilot in downtown Atlanta (right). Andrea (Laurie Holden) comforts her sister Amy (Bell) as she dies after a walker attack on their campsite (far right).

RISKY BUSINESS

SORTING OUT THE WALKERS

In *TWD*, zombies are called everything but: biters, rotters, empties. Some names refer to specific specimens. Here's our danger ranking, from the ones you can let inside your bunker to the surefire killers.

PETS 💀

"You take away their arms so they can't grab ya. You take away their jaws so they can't bite ya. Take away their ability to eat, they lose interest in doing so." —Milton

FLOATERS 💀💀

"Looks like we've got us a swimmer." —Dale

LURKERS 💀💀💀

"The first time I saw a walker, it was just half a body, snapping at me from the ground, and my first inclination wasn't to kill it. But what the world is out there isn't what you saw on TV. It is much, much worse, and it changes you." —Rick

ROAMERS 💀💀💀💀

"The only thing that keeps you from becoming a monster is killing." —Carol

WALKER HERDS 💀💀💀💀💀

"If one of them even so much as brushes a hand against your door [where you are hiding] and another one sees that, mistakes that as an attempt to get in—it's over." —Eugene

ANDREW LINCOLN Q&A

Rick Shoots a Zombie Girl

It was the very first scene of the very first episode, "Days Gone Bye," and it set the tone for everything to follow. Rick Grimes finds postapocalyptic carnage on the road, but what he discovers down the hill by an abandoned gas station is even more horrifying—a little girl with bunny slippers and a teddy bear, who also happens to be a zombie. When Rick shot that little girl in the face, everyone immediately understood that this show came with a set of brand-new rules. *Entertainment Weekly*'s Dalton Ross spoke to Andrew Lincoln about that famous scene and his famous father-in-law (Ian Anderson from Jethro Tull), who watched the entire thing go down. —D. R.

This is the first kill of yours we see onscreen. Was it your first kill of filming as well?
The first kill was actually the first day, which was Bicycle Girl. That was the very first thing that we shot. I can vividly remember it being so extraordinary and weird.

This opener was the second week of filming because my father-in-law was playing in town, and he came and visited the set with my mother-in-law and sat behind [director] Frank Darabont for the whole day. Frank is this huge Jethro Tull fan, and I was so in my own space trying to get the scene right that I didn't introduce them. And Frank has never forgiven me. They're even in a photograph together, and I haven't introduced them. It was the most ill-mannered moment of my whole life—with my in-laws and my new ingenious director. I'm still haunted by it.

What was it like when you arrived on-set for this scene and saw all those burned-out cars and trucks on the road?
I remember coming up and seeing this turned-over Mack truck and thinking, "Holy s---, there's been a f---ing accident!" And then someone was like, "No, you're in the right place. This is your set." That was the beginning of realizing the scale of the show, so walking through that gas station setup was just thrilling. It was the most incredibly immersive experience—and terrifying. And that set the tone and the bar for what that first season was all about. It was extraordinary. It was lots of big expansive setting-up of that world, and that's what I've always seen that first season as being—a man wakes up into a new world. So there was a great ambition in set design and scale that I don't think we've really backed away from much.

Frank Darabont said that the opening teaser serves as a mission statement for the entire series. Do you agree?
I absolutely agree. I loved working with Frank and I remember him [showing me the teaser later], and I just started laughing. I was so shocked by what had happened and how he had cut it together. I said, "Is this the actual thing that is going out?" And he said "Yep." And I went, "Oh my Lord!" And he went, "Yeah, we're trying to tell a story." And I went, "Well, that's it!" You don't need to know any more than that. It expresses in a very short period of time exactly what the show is. And what the world is. And the extremities of the world. I can't think of a more impactful, shocking, thrilling and terrifying beginning. We're horror, and we're not apologetic about it. And we're trying to be emotional. And it's not what you think you're watching. All of those crumbs are fed to you very quickly and effectively.

What sort of interactions did you have with Addy Miller, who played the zombie girl?
Addy was amazing, and the makeup was phenomenal. I had not met her without all of that, so I was just greeted with this terrifying apparition. I had been quite solitary. I really hadn't spoken to anybody, just because of the nature of the story. So I just thought, well, this is a pretty awkward moment because I'm going to have to get a .357 Magnum and shoot this girl in about 30 minutes so I better introduce myself. And I said, "Look, I'm really sorry about all of this and I hope you

@theaddymiller

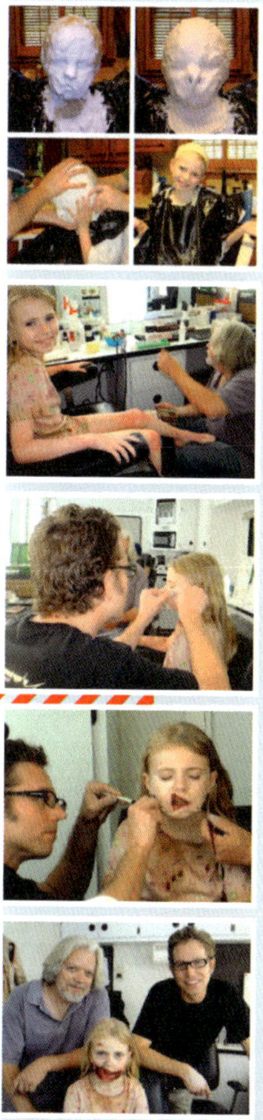

don't mind that I'm going to have to shoot you." And I was really upset by this because it was the nature of the scene, and I was kind of distressed anyway by the whole world. And she was like, "I'm fine; just get on with it." And she was 8 or 9 years old at this point and telling me, "C'mon, man, get to work. We're professionals here."

So she was completely comfortable with the entire idea. And I was the one trying to apologize for the next hour, and she was magnificent. I just remember looking over at my in-laws at one point, and they looked gleeful but also extremely confused and disturbed. And I just thought, that's what we're trying to do. There you go. Welcome to the family!

THE LITTLEST ZOMBIE The drool from 10-year-old Addy Miller's walker-reveal from the series premiere is real; she was unable to swallow while in makeup (opposite). **PREP TIME** Prior to arriving on set, Miller went through extensive prep at "zombie camp," including head and teeth molds and mock fittings. SFX supervisor Greg Nicotero oversaw the makeup, creating a fake set of braces. Pictured are Garrett Immel and Andy Schoneberg, both of Nicotero's KNB EFX Group, who applied the prostheses to Addy over the course of two and a half hours (top eight images). **PLEASED TO EAT YOU** Miller and Lincoln greet each other for the first time before the shoot (above).

PHOTOGRAPH BY MICHAEL MULLER

The Dirty Half Dozen

Only 6 characters have survived through 6 seasons. Now the actors who play them sit down to discuss the past, the future and the tricky art of staying alive **BY DALTON ROSS**

Death is everywhere in the zombie apocalypse. But Andrew Lincoln (Rick), Chandler Riggs (Carl), Steven Yeun (Glenn), Melissa McBride (Carol), Norman Reedus (Daryl) and Lennie James (Morgan) were there at the beginning in season 1, and their characters were still alive and kicking at the end of season 6. We sat down to discuss who was initially scared of whom, how they felt about the dismissal of the man who gave them their jobs and how much longer they plan to keep battling the undead.

ENTERTAINMENT WEEKLY An absurd number of people have perished in terrible ways on this show. Why are you guys so lucky?

NORMAN REEDUS That's a good question. There's a certain story that we're telling, and part of that story involves loss. I don't know if there's anything in particular about any of us and why we're still here; I think we're just part of that story.

ANDREW LINCOLN [*To Melissa McBride*] You had a close shave in season 3.

MELISSA McBRIDE I feel like I always have a close shave.

LINCOLN Yeah, but do you remember, with Sarah Wayne Callies [who played Lori]? She fought for you.

McBRIDE She did? I didn't hear that.

LINCOLN Did you not know?

McBRIDE I didn't know that.

LINCOLN It was the episode when Lori and T-Dog die. But for a few weeks it was going to be Carol and Lori. And Sarah, in her good grace and class, stepped in and said, "That's a terrible mistake." And so she knew that she was going, but she fought for you to stay.

Melissa McBride, Lennie James, Norman Reedus, Chandler Riggs, Andrew Lincoln and Steven Yeun, photographed at San Diego Comic-Con in 2015.

BEFORE THE APOCALYPSE Andrew Lincoln starred opposite Keira Knightley in 2003's rom-com *Love Actually*; Steven Yeun appeared as Sheldon's ex-roommate in *The Big Bang Theory*; and Lennie James's decades-long career included *Snatch*, the TV series *Jericho* and the film *Lucky Break* (shown).

McBRIDE I did not know that. I'm going to faint. Get her on the phone!

EW That speaks to the family you guys have that Sarah is not sitting there fighting for herself to stay on the show, but she's fighting for another actor whom she has respect for.

REEDUS That happens a lot on the show. We get word of something, and everyone rallies to change people's minds. It happens all the time.

EW Have there been instances where any of you have seen a showrunner's name pop up on your phone and think you're getting that call telling you your time is up?

STEVEN YEUN I think that happens every single time.

LENNIE JAMES I got that the other day! Exactly that. We were all out together, which made it even more funny, and a couple of other people had been walking off, talking on their phones kind of heatedly in the corners. And then I got a phone call, and I looked at my phone and it was [showrunner Scott M. Gimple], and I was like, "What?!" I called him back, and actually it was a conversation about somebody else, but my first thought was, "Is this the conversation where he tells me I'm dead? Where he says, 'Thanks for finally coming back, but actually, we're done with you—now move on'?"

EW Getting back to when you all lost Sarah Wayne Callies on the show—Chandler, I remember she felt very protective of you, and not just as your onscreen mother but your on-set mother as well. You were just turning 13 at the time, so being so young, what was that like for you?

CHANDLER RIGGS Depressing. It was hard for both me and Sarah to go through that scene, because it was a two-day scene that we shot, and it just felt so repetitive, over and over and over again. It felt like it got drawn out so much, but everyone's gone through it.

EW Andrew, what's it been like to watch Chandler grow from a young kid to a young man on this show over the past 5½ years?

LINCOLN It's been a privilege. I mean, I've spent probably more time with him than my actual son, sadly. That just shows how terrible a parent I am. [*Turns to Riggs*] You looked like a Cabbage Patch Kid when we first got together, and now you're this young man. I'm hugely fond of everybody, but I love doing scenes with Chandler. There is something incredibly powerful about having this relationship, also just the way that they're telling this story for this young man. It's a frightening story of trauma and loss and how this boy turns into this young adult.

EW I'm sure every death is crushing in its own way, but is there a particular cast member's leaving that really affected you the most?

YEUN I remember Jon Bernthal [who played Shane] leaving was huge. It kind of changed how the show functioned. Jeff DeMunn [Dale] leaving, same thing. Sarah, same thing. Laurie Holden [Andrea], same thing. Scott Wilson [Hershel] leaving, it was just massive. Everybody leaving was devastating because they set the tone on how the show continues to function.

EW Lennie, being here at the beginning, leaving and then coming back, what has changed? How is working on this show different now?

JAMES There was a real fear when we were doing the pilot that it was not a vampire show so it was probably not going to get picked up. Zombies were a whole different

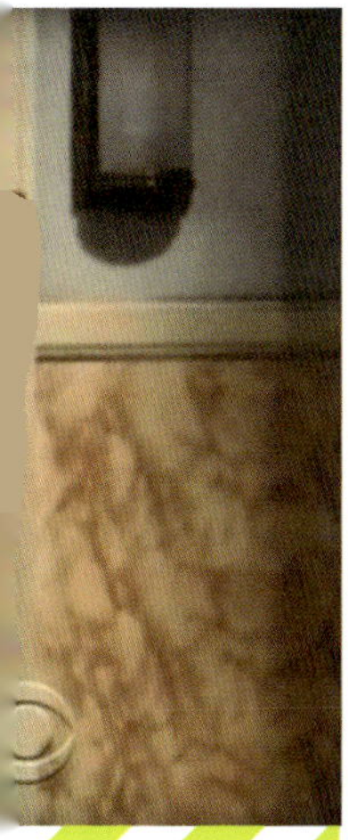

> "ZOMBIES WERE A WHOLE DIFFERENT KIND OF BEAST. . . . IT WAS LIKE YOU WERE GOING TO THE MOON"
>
> —LENNIE JAMES (MORGAN)

kind of beast. At that time it was like you were going to the moon. You were kind of flying blind and didn't even have a sense that we would be doing a second season, let alone a sixth one. We were lucky if anybody would deign to talk to us when we were doing the pilot, where now it is a behemoth, and that's been an adjustment for me.

EW Lennie, what was it like coming back for season 6 full-time and having to meet regular cast members? Obviously you had worked a lot with Andrew but not with some of the others. What was that whole experience like of being an original yet also new-school at the same time?

JAMES It's weird, really, because it's like coming back to some place that's familiar but not actually knowing your way around. The fact of the matter is, we've got 18 regular characters, and until the finale of season 5 I had spoken to Chandler and Andy and that's it.

LINCOLN And you stabbed me.

JAMES Yeah, and I stabbed you. Well, you kind of deserved it, dude.

YEUN I remember you on the pilot because I was just snooping around at the time.

JAMES But even on the pilot I didn't meet any of you guys.

YEUN I met you. You were very scary.

JAMES I was not scary. Don't tell people I'm scary.

YEUN Jon scared the crap out of me, and you scared the crap out of me. You guys are obviously not mean people, but I remember walking into the hair trailer, and Jon had his two dogs, and I'm like, "Hey, guys!" And he's like [*mumbles, imitating Bernthal*]. And then for you I was just like, "Hey, how are you doing? My name is Steven." And you were in character, and I was just like, oh, it's going to suck here. [*Everyone laughs*]

LINCOLN You know why everybody was like that? Because we'd heard about you fainting in your first shot.

YEUN I did not faint!

LINCOLN And we were like, oh…he just came over from the West Coast.

YEUN Did not faint. Did not faint.

EW That's his story and he's sticking to it.

YEUN It's garbage.

EW Which character do you all think has changed the most—because I could make cases for a few of them?

REEDUS I think Carol. Daryl used to look after Carol. Now it's a whole other ball game. Now she's so complex. Not that she wasn't complex before, but that's two totally different animals.

McBRIDE She feels unpredictable.

REEDUS I remember handing her the pickax in episode 5, and I was kind of just f---ing with Melissa.

McBRIDE You were messing with me so bad.

BEFORE THE APOCALYPSE, CONTINUED
Chandler Riggs capitalized on his *TWD* fame, going on to star in 2014's *Mercy*; Melissa McBride appeared in made-for-TV movies and TV series like *Dawson's Creek*; and Norman Reedus had roles in *Blade II* and *The Boondock Saints* (shown).

REEDUS I was like, "Come on, put more blood on that pickax!" It got a little blood, and then it ended up being like guts and blood all over it, and I remember watching her go at it and I was like, "Oh s---!" Little did I know what that character would turn into.

McBRIDE I didn't know either. I figured she would be dead in two episodes. When I first met Carol, I was very protective of her. I was like, "Don't anybody touch her, don't talk about her." Now it's like, "What would Carol do right now?" That's what I think. At first I'd help her walk along, and then she's like, "Okay, I got it."

EW Original showrunner Frank Darabont brought you all into this world and then was taken off the show a year later by AMC in what has proved to be a pretty contentious dispute. I know that hurt for a lot of you. Was there ever a moment where you said to yourself, "I don't want to keep doing this without him"?

LINCOLN It was the most painful year of my career.

REEDUS I didn't get to know Frank as well as everybody else. I came in on the third episode, and he was already editing the first episode, and I kind of met him a little later. I've always been a huge fan of his and grateful that he created this part for me, and I owe him a ton. I remember he came back and he directed a portion of an episode where I come and I save IronE [Singleton, who played T-Dog] on the freeway, and it was my first time to be directed by Frank, and I was superexcited. I'm always trying to be filthy on the show, but the makeup artist said, "That's enough dirt." But Frank was like, "Dirtier!" and I'm like, "I love this guy." He's super f---ing cool, and I wish I had more time with him, to be honest.

EW Melissa, you had worked with Frank on *The Mist* before this.

McBRIDE Yeah, and that was a blast to work with him on. It was just a short day-player role, and I never thought I'd hear another thing and didn't anticipate that I would. I didn't really know him that well, and even going into *The Walking Dead*, he came to set and at the CDC was the first time I had an opportunity to talk to him and thank him, and I did. I turned around and he was gone. It's just like he was this elusive person that...

EW He was the mist.

McBRIDE Yeah, kind of like that. And then when that happened, it was awkward—so awkward, and a little heartbreaking, to say the least. But it was a gift, and it's still a gift, you know? He's a creative force, and I feel very blessed and indebted to him.

EW *Game of Thrones* set a record for most Emmy wins ever in a season, and I know a lot of you love that show, but does it ever make you wonder why your show does not get that same awards-show respect?

LINCOLN I said to Norman once, "If and when the Emmy comes, I will go, 'You know, I used to think awards were divisive and wrong, and then I got one, and now they're strangely moving and true.' " [*Laughs*] But I do think we have been hindered by a genre that has not been looked favorably upon. It's always been seen as a B-movie sort of area, and even when we spoke about season 1 and what Frank's intentions were, everybody said serialized horror will never work.

RIGGS They said that?

LINCOLN Yeah! And now I see on TV, everything is a horror movie that's coming out! But this is not a horror movie, it's a story. It's a story in the same way that it's just

"WHAT [SCOTT GIMPLE] IS ABLE TO DO WITH 18 PRINCIPAL CHARACTERS ...IS BREATHTAKING"

—ANDREW LINCOLN (RICK)

about people trying to do something, hopefully that's engaging and different. I would love for Scott [Gimple] to be recognized. That's my beef. He's a perfectionist, which is why he doesn't sleep. What he's able to do with 18 principal characters and reinventing the show continually is breathtaking, and I would love that. That's my pitch, anyway.

EW Let me ask you all about the other side of this. You have such a passionate fan base, but also a very opinionated fan base. How much do you pay attention to any of the negativity out there?

REEDUS I mean, you can't not see it. Some people out there, all they do all day is they sit behind their computer and they just bash you. I've gotten to a point where I pay attention but don't really pay attention.

RIGGS I also feel like our show is, in some weird way, a precursor to Netflix and streaming. I don't want to say this, but it's tougher to watch this show week by week.

YEUN I know what you're saying.

RIGGS If you binge-watch it, you will see the payoff. It's just annoying that people can't comment on the whole thing. Instead, they have to pick apart each moment.

LINCOLN Yeah, but without that argument and that dialogue, the fan base wouldn't be as big. You know what I mean?

REEDUS True.

LINCOLN And all it shows is passion. That's just a commitment. They're in the story and that energy is good, and that energy fuels other energy, and it makes people watch it.

EW I know you all consider *The Walking Dead* the best job in the world, but do you ever think about how much longer you want to keep doing this?

RIGGS I was talking to Andy about this because I can't imagine this guy doing it for much longer. [*Looking at Lincoln*] Like, with your kids and everything, just being gone for so long from your home, year after year. I always ask him, "How long do you think you're going to keep on doing this?" Because I'm on it as long as he's on it.

LINCOLN What did I say?

RIGGS I think you just said, "As long as Scott's still on the show."

LINCOLN Yeah, I think that's it. He holds the cards, that guy, because, in my opinion, the last three years have been some of the finest storytelling that we've attempted. I think he is the person to ask that question to.... We may get flak if we stop the show, but I hope that when it finishes, we've done it right, so in maybe five years' time we'll be forgiven for leaving, and they'll realize that we left it when it was just right. It would be disingenuous to the fans to keep rolling it out for another three or four seasons just because we could.

SEASON 2

...
I'M SO SORRY.

YOU WERE RIGHT.

Battle of Cain & Abel

A new showrunner, compelling cast members, a farm overflowing with secrets: Season 2 kept viewers riveted. At its decaying heart was Rick and best friend Shane's struggle for dominance

WELL BEFORE FANS WERE TREATED TO THE onscreen thrills of season 2, the series experienced its fair share of drama behind the scenes. Showrunner Frank Darabont, credited with shepherding the series to television, was abruptly pushed out after disagreements with AMC network execs only a few days after taking a promotional victory lap at 2011's San Diego Comic-Con.

"It's definitely not easy," Robert Kirkman said at the time. "Frank was a very big part of this show from the get-go." No official reason was given, but rumors swirled about a budget dispute, quickly denied by AMC president Charlie Collier, who insisted, "It wasn't budget-related at all."

Fans and critics were also nervous, but it was Darabont himself who took his removal the hardest. He claimed to have stopped watching the show entirely and two years later filed a lawsuit against AMC, accusing the network of breaching his contract and

BARN RAISING Carl and Rick defend against a herd of walkers. Comic pages from *The Walking Dead* No. 11; art by Charlie Adlard and tones by Cliff Rathburn (previous spread).

denying him millions in profits.

Back on-set, Darabont's second-in-command, Glen Mazzara, rose to the top job and acknowledged the challenge ahead. "I did have a lot of mixed emotions," he admitted. "Not only was I then terrified about being the guy who could possibly mess up *The Walking Dead,* but I also felt bad for my friend." Luckily the show was on the rise: The high ratings of the first season persuaded the network to increase its season 2 order to 13 episodes.

Meanwhile the dramas onscreen saw Rick's band of survivors leaving Atlanta behind. While looking for Carol's daughter Sophia they discovered a farm hidden in the woods—a potential safe haven. There they found Hershel Greene (Scott Wilson), a stubborn old widower with medical experience and a strong moral compass. Hershel would become a central figure, as would his daughters Maggie (Lauren Cohan) and young Beth (Emily Kinney).

Close quarters led to new beginnings: Lori's pregnancy became known, and a romance blossomed between Maggie and Glenn. "It's cool to have a beacon of hope and light in this cavern of doom," said Steven Yeun. But it was the simmering feud between Rick and former best friend Shane that defined the survivors' peaceful interlude on Hershel's farm.

On the surface it was an argument about the missing Sophia: Rick insisted the search continue; Shane pragmatically believed that extending the hunt only endangered the rest of the survivors. For Rick, refusing to give up on Sophia meant holding on to his principles. Shane's judgment was wholly overshadowed by his unpredictable behavior and fueled by his all-absorbing jealousy of Rick—who had the wife, family and leadership role Shane had temporarily enjoyed.

Their showdown left Shane dead and Rick changed forever. And everyone learned the grim reality: The infection was already inside them. In the end the group fled the farm and started over on the highway. Except for Andrea—separated from the others, she had a fateful encounter with a mysterious woman wielding a very big sword. —RAY RAHMAN

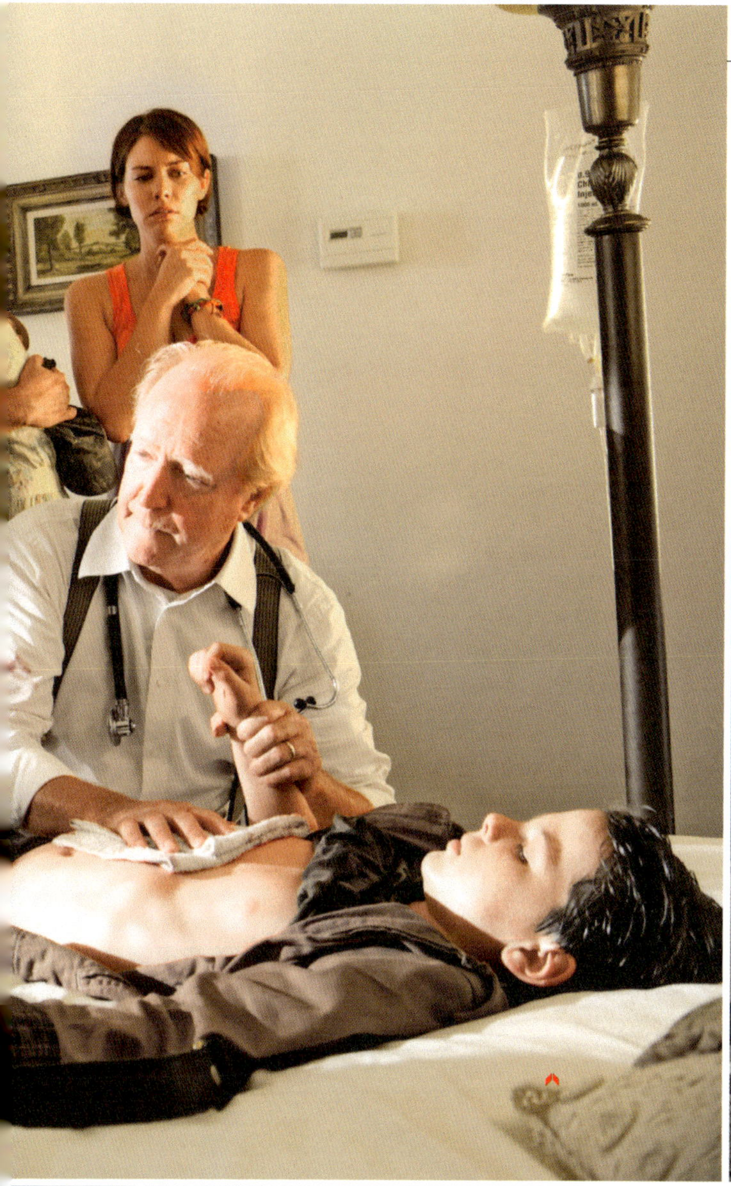

CLOSE ENCOUNTERS From left to right: Shane, Rick, Otis (Pruitt Taylor Vince), Otis's wife, Patricia (Jane McNeill), Maggie (Lauren Cohan), Hershel (Scott Wilson) and Carl, immediately after a hunting accident in the woods (top left). SFX artist Greg Nicotero adds gore to a dummy walker before the cameras begin to roll (top right).

RUN AND GUN Glenn, trapped when he went searching for Hershel, prepares to face off against a human threat (far left). A walker cracks the windshield of Lori's vehicle with its head as she wakes from unconsciousness after her car accident (middle). Delirious from his injuries, Daryl begins to hallucinate his older brother, who's been missing since season 1 (left).

▲ **SIX FEET UNDER** From left to right: Patricia, Hershel, Maggie, Beth (Emily Kinney), Jimmy (James Allen McCune), Glenn, T-Dog, Andrea, Dale (Jeffrey DeMunn), Shane, Rick, Carl, Lori and Daryl mourn their fallen in the aftermath of discovering the barn's grim contents.

▶ **LOVE BITES** Glenn and Maggie in a stolen embrace (right). When the feud between Rick and Shane boils over, the two duke it out in a municipal lot, and Shane topples a motorcycle on Rick (middle). Shane rises again as a walker (far right).

SURVIVAL TACTICS

GETTING BY IN A WALKER WORLD

If anyone can live through the undead and human horrors of Zombiepocalypse, it's Team Rick. Here's some of the grim strategies they've developed to outsmart the killer hordes.

EVERYONE'S ALREADY INFECTED
Rick learned this secret from Dr. Jenner: Everyone will reanimate as a walker, and the survivors need to be ready to put them down.

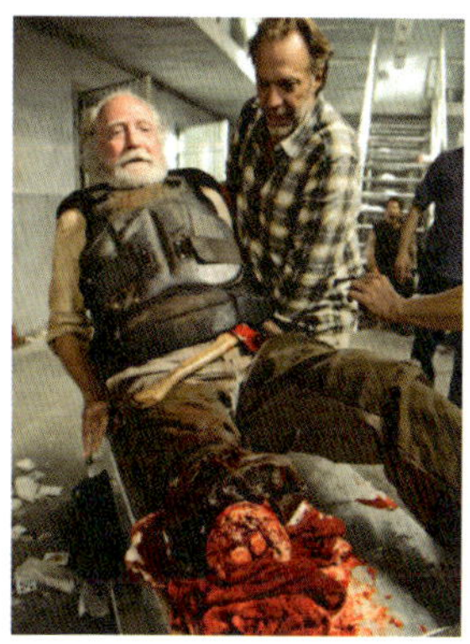

BITES DON'T MEAN IT'S OVER
An untreated bite brings infection, fever and eventually death. But quick action (like an amputation) before the infection spreads might stave off death—*if* you survive the surgery.

NOISE AND LIGHT ATTRACTS
It's one of the first things Rick learns from Morgan. So while in unknown territory, keep it dark and quiet. Stealth weapons, such as a crossbow or sword, are preferable to guns.

"THEY SMELL DEAD, WE DON'T"
Rick and Glenn slather their clothes with walker guts and gore to test this olfactory theory in a first-season gross-out moment.

SCOTT M. GIMPLE Q&A

Zombie Sophia Walks Out of the Barn

The Walking Dead's blending of heart and horror has never been more powerful than when the anguished search for Sophia, which stretched throughout the first half of season 2, came to a close. When Carol's daughter emerged in zombie form from Hershel's barn in "Pretty Much Dead Already," Shane and the others stood in stunned silence. Then Rick finished the job, putting down the young walker. Scott M. Gimple, who wrote the episode and now serves as the series' showrunner, reveals what it was like on-set, how the climax was partly inspired by *Seinfeld* and what it meant for the evolution of the show. —D. R.

What can you tell me about the shooting of this pivotal scene?

I remember the day building and building with emotion. A lot of horrible things have happened on *The Walking Dead*, with this story of these characters going through an increasingly deteriorating world, but this was one of the big ones. Rick wanted to be the guy who would look for the little girl who was lost. Shane was the realist who didn't. Michelle MacLaren directed it, and when she called cut after Shane gave that speech before he shoots the walker that Rick is holding, somebody on the camera crew uttered a very supportive profanity with his performance. It was just a remarkable performance by Jon Bernthal.

I had designed the script like an episode of *Seinfeld* in a lot of ways. All of these disparate stories crashing together at the end. So everybody had a story that tied them up in some way emotionally, and it all came together in this moment. Meanwhile they find out about this threat in the barn right under their noses. It was just one of those moments that defined the show because it had these spectacular walkers coming out and this violence that was very much contextualized with a heartbreaking act.

This isn't a kick-ass thing they're doing. This is somebody saying that the world is dead, which was Shane, and to be a realist. It was almost like shooting down idealism. Emotionally the energy felt like it changed and that things have heightened. It was a remarkable day. It was all these different parts of what makes a show come together in this perfect moment. It's the kind of stuff I've been trying to shoot forever since.

There was a lot of bellyaching going on among fans during the search for Sophia, with people saying "This is taking way too long." But then everyone loved the payoff, right?

That's one of the lessons I learned: The audience wants to know things sooner rather than later. In that case I think if they knew sooner, it would have been denied some of the impact. The audience, in some ways, had to suffer along with the characters. It made them bound in some way so that when you had that final moment, it wasn't just the characters feeling that. The audience felt it more because they had put in that time on that search.

It's riskier TV, I guess, because you're asking the audience to go through some hard stuff to elicit an even bigger emotion and an even bigger payoff at the end. I loved it. It was a great experience doing that.

Why is Rick the one who has to put that bullet in Sophia?

Because it was about him changing. Because it was about him accepting some realities. So many seasons are about Rick's transformation, but this was a big one. He was the one strong enough to do this. Nobody else stepped up to do it. He did. If he was strong enough to look for the little girl, he was strong enough to put her out of her misery when she was found to be a walker.

It's always a big day on-set when it's someone's death scene. How was that for the young Madison Lintz, who played Sophia?

She was remarkable and was an incredible pro. In many ways she was and is an old soul. Madison had to come out as a walker essentially onstage. The entire cast for the most part was lined up in front of her and then all of the cameras all around her.

It was so theatrical that she basically stepped out from behind the curtain. She came out and it was horrible, so she did her job incredibly well. The acting in that scene was heartbreaking. It was one of those days where everybody was topping one another in the performances. Madison absolutely did that. For seven episodes to crash into this 10 seconds, it's an incredibly important moment.

WRITER TO SHOWRUNNER Known for his intricate, character-driven scripts, Gimple was installed as the series' third showrunner at the start of season 4. He later made some hard decisions, defending character deaths as a means of maintaining realism and establishing stakes. "You do what's best for the story, first and foremost," says Gimple. "It's scary to lose characters and a tool in your toolbox, but so much of what we do on this show is about loss."

Making of a Zombie

Want to know what it's like to turn into a walker? *EW*'s Dalton Ross found out when he enlisted as an extra in the season 2 premiere of *The Walking Dead*, braving Atlanta's brutal heat, a visit to the makeup studio of SFX guru Greg Nicotero and the real-life actor problem of having one's scene cut. He lived to tell the tale.

BEING A ZOMBIE has its drawbacks. First off, they don't tend to make great conversationalists. (Enough with the moaning already!) Hygiene is certainly an issue. Worst of all, the situation is permanent. But what if you could be a zombie for a day, to get a taste—no pun intended—of how the undead other half lives? For the season 2 premiere, I did just that, venturing down to Atlanta to volunteer my services on *The Walking Dead*'s set.

My first stop is at wardrobe, where I am promptly handed an enormous bloodstained suit, which makes me look like a cross between a homeless person and *Stop Making Sense*-era David Byrne. My shoes are tagged with the words "Chad Sanders," so I choose to adopt that as my zombie name. Of course, the real fun happens in the makeup chair. Makeup guru Greg Nicotero and his team have 35 zombies to gorify today. Some just get a "paint job," which is a liberal application of dirt, grime and blood, while others get the "hero zombie" treatment, which means an assortment of prosthetic gashes, demon-eye contact lenses and phony rotted teeth.

I sit down in the chair of makeup artist Andy Schoneberg, and the transformation begins. My wound du jour is a huge bloody mess on my forehead, and while it looks cool as hell, it also has me wondering—what sort of lamebrain was Chad Sanders, anyway? I mean, I can see getting bitten on the arm, leg or even neck—but the forehead? How does that even happen? That's just poor zombie defense skills, is what that is. Great, I'm playing a moron.

An hour and a half later, after having disgusting yellow and black fluid squirted all over my teeth, and hellacious orange contacts inserted into my eyes, I'm ready for action. The scene we're shooting involves a horde of ghouls descending upon an abandoned Shane (Jon Bernthal). Although it means multiple takes at multiple angles for multiple hours, it is a full-on blast every single time. After all, how often in life are people feeding you instructions such as "Attack him like you want to rip his flesh off!"?

In between takes, the zombies devour the one thing they crave in the 95° heat even more than flesh: Gatorade. Several also light up cigarettes. (I suppose if you're already dead, lung cancer is the least of your worries.) Finally, 12 hours later, we gear up for one last run, chasing Bernthal over the course of a few hundred yards. It's brutal, intense and gnarly, but when the director yells "Cut!" for the last time, the actor and my zombie brethren exchange high fives and congratulations all around. In my exhausted euphoria, little do I realize that my zombie life is still in danger, for there is one other surefire way to kill a member of the walking dead—cut his scene out of the show. And sure enough, this entire day ends up on the editing-room floor. Poor Chad Sanders; dude just can't catch a break.

"YOU KNOW SOME GIRLS LIKE TO PLAY BARBIES? WELL, US OLD GUYS LIKE TO PLAY ZOMBIES"

—FRANK DARABONT

LIVING THE DEAD LIFE (from top) Makeup artist Andy Schoneberg applies several foam latex prosthetics. After blending, grime and fake blood are added—even on the teeth. Robert Kirkman faces one of his creations on the set. Lunch is served (salad, naturally) during the 12-hour shoot (left).

PHOTOGRAPHS BY GENE PAGE

SEASON 3

Cutting to the Quick

Brothers reunited, then lost; a community controlled by terror, another by fear; and new friends, greeted with suspicion. *TWD*'s third season explored the horrors that hide in the human soul

THERE ARE FEW METAPHORS MORE POTENT than a prison. After an emotionally draining stay on the farm and months on the road, Rick and Daryl stumble upon the large, imposing West Georgia Correctional Facility, which would serve as the group's new home and fortress. Freedom, they believed, could be found in jail.

But life had other plans for the survivors. Season 3 bid an early farewell to Lori, who was unable to pull through an emergency C-section. (The baby, however, lived.) "*The Walking Dead* has broken more hearts than I've ever seen," actress Sarah Wayne Callies says of Lori's demise. "You give your love to a character...and then—poof—there's a hole where they used to be." For the series it was a poignant focal point; for fans it was a precedent-setting tragedy that proved no one on the show is guaranteed to stick around.

HEADS OR TAILS After leaving Andrea behind at Woodbury, Michonne (Danai Gurira) divides and conquers outside the prison. Comic pages from *The Walking Dead* No. 34; art by Charlie Adlard and tones by Cliff Rathburn (previous spread).

The cast also received some new blood. Michonne, the fierce warrior beloved by book fans, lived up to expectations. Wisely, Zimbabwean-American Danai Gurira, who plays Michonne, underwent sword training for the role. "The essence of the character—her personality, her motives, everything that makes Michonne Michonne—is intact from the comics," says Robert Kirkman, who also assured viewers they'd "get to know her a lot faster than comic-book readers did."

Other additions were a new kind of terror: the human variety. "The zombies are always a huge problem, but they have become a known quantity," showrunner Glen Mazzara said at the time. "What's unknown is the darkness of humanity and the evil that other people can do."

As the dictator of a fortified town called Woodbury, the Governor (English actor David Morrissey) ruthlessly maintained power by any means necessary—including an all-out war against Rick's prison camp. The good guys prevailed but not without casualties, including Andrea and Daryl's brother Merle.

There were losses behind the camera as well. Before the season had even finished airing, Mazzara announced in a joint statement with the network that he would be leaving the series due to "a difference of opinion about where the show should go moving forward." *TWD* was losing its second showrunner in as many years. The move left many wondering why AMC's highest-rated title was beset by so much backstage drama—and what the change might mean for the show's future.

Despite the departure of two showrunners, the hit drama continued to shatter ratings records, and in 2012 *TWD*'s brand had spread as fast as the zombie virus it depicts, spinning off a companion recap show, *Talking Dead*; multiple video games; and an exhibit at Universal Studios' theme parks. "It's definitely cool to see *The Walking Dead* grow into what it has grown into," said creator Kirkman in 2012. "But...I do feel a responsibility to make sure it doesn't get too out of hand. There are things like perfume and energy drinks that I'm like, 'That's going too far.'" —RAY RAHMAN

▲ **IT DOESN'T ABODE WELL**
Top left: The crew susses out the prison during the season premiere. Top right: During the explosive "Welcome to the Tombs," the residents of the prison defend their new home from the Governor.

◄ **WHAT DREAMS MAY COME**
Far left: The Governor grooms his undead daughter Penny (Kylie Szymanski). Middle: After Penny's death the Governor leads the people of Woodbury in a retaliatory attack on the prison. Left: Maggie faces off against a guard.

▲
BRAWL IN THE FAMILY The Dixon boys band together when the Governor forces Merle to prove his loyalty inside his undead-gladiator pit (top).

▶
ARRESTING DEVELOPMENTS
Right: While on a supply run, Rick encounters now-mentally-unstable friend Morgan Jones (Lennie James). Middle: Steven Yeun (Glenn) takes a break between scenes. Far right: Rick's hallucinations, including those of his dead wife, begin to impact his leadership while at the prison.

EASTER EGGS

WHAT YOU MAY HAVE MISSED

The series is packed with quirky cameos and clever allusions. Here are our favorite under-the-radar references. How many did you catch?

LIKE A PRAYER
Father Gabriel Stokes's church is stuffed with zombie…allusions. Above the altar is a passage from the Bible, John 6:54: "He who eats my flesh and drinks my blood has eternal life." On the hymn board are references to other quotes, including Matthew 27:52 ("And the tombs were opened") and Revelation 9:6 ("They shall desire to die, and death fleeth from them").

COMIC TIMING
Before Robert Kirkman made it big on *TWD*'s comics, he worked on *Invincible* with Cory Walker, Ryan Ottley and Bill Crabtree, a comic series that featured a main character obsessed with an in-world comic called Science Dog. Carl Grimes is spotted multiple times wearing a Science Dog T-shirt and paging through comic books—including *Invincible*.

***BREAKING* DEAD**
References to AMC's other blockbuster show abound—including a glimpse of Walt's blue meth—leading fans to theorize that *TWD* is set in *Breaking Bad*'s future. Glenn's getaway car in season 1 is the same model purchased by Walter White.

HEAD SHOTS
Season 6's "Not Tomorrow Yet" featured a sneak cameo of director Greg Nicotero—as one of the severed heads. The gruesome prop was a hit on-set. "Norman kept saying he wanted the heads when we were done shooting," Nicotero added.

NORMAN REEDUS Q&A

Daryl Mourns Merle

He's been called *The Walking Dead*'s resident badass, but noted tough guy Daryl Dixon (played by Norman Reedus) also has a very tender side. That vulnerability was laid bare in a heartbreaking scene in the episode "This Sorrowful Life" in which Daryl not only discovered his brother Merle (Michael Rooker) had turned into a walker, but then had to finish the job—mixing stabs and sobs as he tearfully killed his zombified sibling in one of the show's most devastating moments. We spoke to Reedus about his preparation for that emotional day of filming, and what it meant for both him and his character. —D. R.

What do you remember most about filming this incredible scene?

I remember when we got that script and reading it. And just thinking how hard this day was going to be and how I wanted to pay respect to Michael as an actor. I was a big fan of his even before the show, and this was at a time when he and I were really starting to hit it off. We were really starting to bond and become good friends, and we were having dinner together quite a bit. He really was like a big brother. That day was so hard. It was a very intense, very sad, emotional day for everyone involved.

It's really a tragic end to this complicated relationship between brothers.

I had to play that out as the brother of Merle, and what those two characters have gone through up to that point. And it is also about the changes in Daryl and how he's no longer under the thumb of his brother. His brother had recognized that he was starting to become his own man now, and it was Merle's previous absence that actually made that happen. So I just remember shooting that and [director Greg Nicotero] said, "You're not just stabbing him to kill him. You go on a rage and stab him, and you're stabbing the circumstances. You're hating the world at this point and what the world is now, and what the world's led you to have to do."

You had a Willie Nelson song queued up before you filmed that scene, right?

Yeah, I played it over and over. We use music a lot of the times to get in the right state, and a lot of times it's not the song that you think you would play. You would imagine I would play a really sad, depressing song, but I played a very uplifting Willie Nelson song because it reminded me of something. It was a song my dad used to like. I remember him playing it when I was a kid. It could lead to a happy moment, which led me to a sad moment, but sometimes it's not the obvious choice.

This scene is about Daryl having to say goodbye to his brother and their whole very complicated relationship. It's interesting how you used your relationship with your father to help you connect the dots.

After you do this a while, you learn things about yourself, and sometimes to go to a sad place you've got to go remember something happy that you lost. I lost my father too young and I was dealt a bad hand, and that's what I thought about for that scene where my brother's taken from me. It is all connected in a weird way.

Is this the hardest scene you've ever had to film on the show?

I've filmed so many hard ones—hard in different ways. Carrying Beth out [of the hospital] in season 5 was hard. I just looked at her and went away and cried for a long time and then came out and did it. But that was different because I didn't want to break down on camera, I wanted it to look like I had already been crying for half an hour. They're all different, and you approach them in different ways.

It's interesting because some actors would really look forward to doing a big scene like that to show off their chops. Were you feeling that way on the day you did the Merle

scene? Or were you kind of dreading it, knowing the places you were going to have to go emotionally to pull it off, while also saying goodbye to Rooker?

I hated that day. I hated it. I'm not one of those people that can turn it on and just cry a flood of tears and then just turn it off and go have a coffee and be cool again. I go to bed thinking about it and I have a knot in my stomach, and I wake up and I don't want to go to work. I don't want to do it, and we're about to film it, and everything floods to the front and I'm just miserable. I mean, I have to get miserable to play miserable, and that day was miserable for everybody. I think that's what made that scene so good.

THE NEW GUY IN TOWN It's ironic that Daryl Dixon has become such a fan favorite, considering he wasn't even supposed to be on *The Walking Dead* to begin with. Reedus's audition impressed the producers so much they created an original role that didn't exist in the comics—a badass with a heart of gold. "Norman brings a cool factor," said season 3 showrunner Glen Mazzara. "He kicks ass. He's fearless. We've seen him heartbroken. [The character is] emotional, but he is afraid to show that. We've never seen him afraid of the physical danger, and yet we've seen him pull away when something becomes too emotionally painful."

1
GOLDEN AGE
Cameraman Mike Satrazemis goes in for a close-up of the then-13-year-old Chandler Riggs. "It's pretty wild to see his growth," says Yeun of his costar. "To see someone turn from an actual kid to a young man and a teenager is pretty remarkable—and to see how he's grown as an actor as well."

2
TRAILER GAMES
Letters from a young fan named Sean Jacoby adorn Yeun's trailer wall, while the mirror holds mementos of him and Lauren Cohan (Maggie) riding horses on-set. "This is from the day we had our first little sex scene," he reveals. When it comes to fan mail, however, Yeun is no match for costar Norman Reedus: "His room is absurd, with wall-to-wall Daryl Dixon paraphernalia everywhere."

3
BAD MOON RISING
Night shoots are a regular event on the set of *The Walking Dead*. "As a photographer, to shoot this stuff, it's a gold mine," says Yeun about the location. "It's a dream."

4
SAYING GOODBYE
"I don't know why we haven't learned our lesson that actors on this show do come and go, so it would only behoove us to not get close," says Yeun about those like Lew Temple (second from left, with Cohan, Melissa McBride, Emily Kinney and Andrew Lincoln). Temple's character Axel was killed in the third season. "Whenever we lose them, it's pretty rough. I'm waiting for a case study in 10 years that shows the cast and crew with full-blown depression."

Steven Yeun's Personal POV

When he's not on-camera shooting zombies as survivor Glenn, the actor is training his own lens on his costars, the grips, the sets and more. Here, Yeun shares his favorite behind-the-scenes snaps from the third season. **BY DALTON ROSS**

4

"ANY SANE HUMAN WHO DIDN'T KNOW WHAT OUR SHOW WAS ABOUT WOULD FREAK THE F--- OUT"

—STEVEN YEUN

1

3

1

MONSTER APPETITE
Yeun says he doesn't flinch anymore at eating lunch alongside pus-spewing zombies. "We're so desensitized now. It's like, 'Oooh, you got his tongue to do that? That's solid!'" he says. "And then you go back to your chicken fillet."

2

UNSUNG HEROES
"These are our grips," says Yeun. "This is the backbone. This is the right arm and the left arm and maybe all the legs to our show. They're scaling trees, they're climbing roofs, they're carrying 100-lb. crazy s--- around. They're nuts, and they do it with a smile on their faces."

3

DECOMPOSURE
This is one of many zombie dummies lying around on-set. "If you were to extend this picture out, there are bodies on top of bodies on top of bodies," Yeun explains. "And any sane human who didn't know what our show was about would freak the f--- out. And the 'Randoms' tag is hilarious to me—they have so many bodies that they can't even categorize them!"

4

SNOOZE ALARM
As hot as it can be in the Atlanta summer, and as incredible as the prison set can be on the interior, Yeun likes filming outside. "I prefer exteriors. And the reason for that is it's brutal outside and the conditions are rough, but in all honesty, it keeps you up, awake and present. The inside has this way of lulling you into comfort. I might be narcoleptic." He adds, "I just fall asleep wherever I can. I'm a pretty tired person all around."

SEASON 4

SWEETWATER
ROAD TRIP
SWEETWATER
420

The Night Shift

There are three constants in the postapocalyptic world: Zombies swarm, characters die, and showrunners change. Scott Gimple stepped up for *TWD*'s darkest, most outré season yet

"THERE ARE A WHOLE LOT OF PEOPLE I DON'T want to let down," newly minted showrunner Scott Gimple said before the fourth season's outset. "I started reading the comic book when it came out, and I [didn't work] on season 1, so I was a fan of the show too. I don't want to let down myself, either." As a writer, Gimple was responsible for a number of episodes beloved by fans (like season 2's "Pretty Much Dead Already," in which Sophia was discovered during Barnageddon, and season 3's "Clear," featuring the return of Lennie James's mentally compromised Morgan)—a promising sign of things to come.

The show quickly evolved under Gimple. Many of the episodes became more character-driven, with a greater emphasis on introspection—something the cast felt could let *The Walking Dead* deepen. "[It's] a beautiful tale of survival that wraps around specific characters but then also

IN THE KICK OF TIME Walkers swarm Daryl inside the liquor store (left). Comic pages from *The Walking Dead* No. 42; art by Charlie Adlard and tones by Cliff Rathburn (previous spread).

shows you the terror and the doom of a wider scope of horrible society," explains Steven Yeun. "If that requires a slower pace here and a wider lens there, I think that's completely fair." In other words, those quieter moments only make the impact even more forceful when everything ultimately goes horribly wrong.

It certainly got very quiet at first. The season opens with the prison transformed into a semi-peaceful commune, complete with a garden full of crops, farm animals and regular mealtimes. Anyone could seek entry to their new community, now led by a council, by answering three simple questions: How many walkers have you killed? How many people? Why?

Their peaceful reprieve didn't last long. Season 4 contained some of the most upsetting moments to date. Carol murders two sick prison residents and burns their bodies, prompting Rick to banish her. Hershel is brutally decapitated at the hands of the Governor, only mere moments before the Governor's own violent end. But perhaps the worst came when Carol heart-wrenchingly executed a girl named Lizzie. Andrew Lincoln calls it "the most controversial episode we've ever attempted." Many started to wonder whether the show had started to rely too much on shock value, but Gimple dismisses that concern. "This was not a story that was sensational. It was something that was very much a part of Carol's story." Melissa McBride concurs, saying of her character, "I think she just did what needed to be done."

The season also welcomed a new trio: the mullet-sporting Eugene (played by Josh McDermitt), a self-professed scientist who claimed to know the cure but needed to get to D.C.; his burly mission-driven partner Abraham (Michael Cudlitz); and their feisty companion Rosita (Christian Serratos). And though the survivors' rushed abandonment of the prison after the Governor's final onslaught had split them into different groups, ultimately their instincts pulled them toward the same place—a seemingly safe community called, ominously enough, Terminus. —RAY RAHMAN

NOT OUT OF THE WOODS YET Carol and Tyreese unite as they escape from the prison (top left). A cameraman captures the reanimation of Pete (Enver Gjokaj) in this behind-the-scenes image (top right).

WHAT PERILS AWAIT When a virulent illness sweeps the prison, Glenn hovers near death's door (far left). The innocuous-looking Terminus rail station hides a dark secret (middle). The Governor, now known as Brian, seizes control of another group of survivors after murdering their leader, his former confidant Martinez (Jose Pablo Cantillo) (left).

CELL BLOCK AND ROLL A torrent of walkers pour over the fences protecting the West Georgia Correctional Facility.

THE RAIL WORLD Executive producer and makeup special-effects artist Greg Nicotero transports a dummy (right). Carl and Michonne bond while following the train tracks to Terminus station (far right).

IT'S SHOW TIME

HEY, WAS THAT IN THE COMICS?

When developing plotlines, characters or settings for the TV show, the producers and writers of *The Walking Dead* sometimes look beyond the original source material

HANDS FREE
Rick Grimes loses his right hand to the Governor in the comics when they meet, but on the show Andrew Lincoln leaves their encounter unscathed. Kirkman later stressed that the decision was due to CGI limitations. "[W]e cheat in the comic because things aren't moving."

SHOWDOWN AT THE FARM
Shane has a meltdown at the end of season 2. In the comics, Rick and Shane face off much earlier—and it's Carl who shoots Shane, plaintively saying afterward, "It's not the same as killing the dead ones, Daddy."

NEW BLOOD
Two of the show's influential characters don't exist in the comic: Daryl Dixon, who first appeared in season 1, and Sasha (Sonequa Martin-Green), introduced in season 3. Both had initially auditioned for other roles.

CDC REVEAL
In the season 1 finale, the band of survivors arrives at Atlanta's CDC, and we learn that the infection has spread worldwide. The fate of the globe is far more uncertain in Kirkman's books; not only do the survivors never make it to the CDC, they are cut off from the rest of the world.

MIKE SATRAZEMIS Q&A

Carol Shoots Lizzie

It might be the most controversial moment in *Walking Dead* history: Carol (Melissa McBride) tells Lizzie (Brighton Sharbino) to "look at the flowers"—and then shoots the young girl in the head. While Carol's heartbreaking decision was driven by necessity, as the unhinged Lizzie had earlier stabbed her sister Mika (Kyla Kenedy), believing she would come back to life, Carol's final solution was startling. The landmark episode was the directorial debut for the show's longtime camera operator and director of photography Mike Satrazemis. Here, he looks back on that pivotal scene. —D.R.

What was your reaction when you first read the script for "The Grove"?
At first it's shocking and horrifying. So I knew it was pretty heavy and intense and a little scary. Having directed [Brighton and Kyla] and worked with them a little bit, I knew who they were, and that made me feel better. But it's very heavy content for two girls who were 9 years old at the time.

Let's get into the scene where Carol tells Lizzie to "look at the flowers" and then puts her down. How did you want to approach this big, pivotal encounter?
We got to this moment, and I [realized I didn't want to] shoot Lizzie falling down. It was crazy. Brighton was like, "Look, I want to die. I'm okay with it. I'm totally fine." I was like, "That's cool, but I don't even want to see you drop on the ground. I'm not really okay with it." I tried one shot [where you see her fall], but I did it only one time, and it was through [the point of view of] Tyreese, where they're just [visible as] two little dots in the distance. That was the only time I ever had her fall over. It was one take, and it was just so heartbreaking.

How did Melissa McBride handle the moment?
I don't know another actress who has an access to so many emotions and to such a depth of the entire human experience. She's one of the greatest actors I've ever worked with and/or seen. So with them, we just let it go. I tried to really pick the cut in advance so we didn't overshoot it, because it's a lot to ask of everybody, and then we brought them out [to the set]. This was such emotional content, so we all talked about creating the atmosphere that's best, so everybody was quiet. So when it was time to roll, [it felt like] the cameras were barely there, and we just shot it.

Was there a discussion of what you could and could not show? Because you have that scene, and you also have the Lizzie and Mika scene where you see Lizzie with the bloody knife and you see Mika's head, but you don't really see much of the stab wound or anything else.
I had to get on the phone for an hour with standards and practices and go through what they thought could be aired. Even when you see Mika on the ground, that's not actually really the actress on the ground. That's a double, so at least I didn't have to dump blood on Kyla while she was pretending to play dead. It was just another girl who was like, "Oh yeah, cool," and then lay down, and we put blood on her. But as far as what could air and what could not, I was told absolutely no way we would ever be able to see her wound in the same shot.

You must have known that this was an episode that was going to get a lot of attention due to the subject matter. Were you worried that people were going to say *The Walking Dead* had gone too far?

Well, the world was talking. I was hearing so much stuff, even a couple of comments at some point about how we may never be able to air this, that they may pull it. But I was always under the belief that if it was told properly, you'd understand it wasn't horror for horror's sake and death for death's sake. We weren't doing it to be flashy, and I tried to really not emphasize any of the gore. It was a story told through Carol's perspective, and you could feel her pain.

GRIM FAREWELL "The Grove" marked the final (living and breathing) appearances of Lizzie Samuels and Mika Samuels. A similar plotline featuring twin boys appeared in *The Walking Dead* No. 61, and showrunner Scott Gimple later confirmed the episode was an adaptation of that incident. The graphic novel featured Carl as the executioner rather than Carol, and the latter's slow evolution from a domestic-abuse victim to a woman in a position of power attracted attention from viewers. "Carol started out with an absence of strength in the face of [her husband] Ed," Gimple said, "and now she's easily one of the strongest characters."

Signs of the Apocalypse

It takes more than zombies and fake blood to bring *The Walking Dead* to life. We got the surprising stories behind the show's best-known weapons and mementos (and a few severed appendages) —DALTON ROSS AND MARC SNETIKER

1

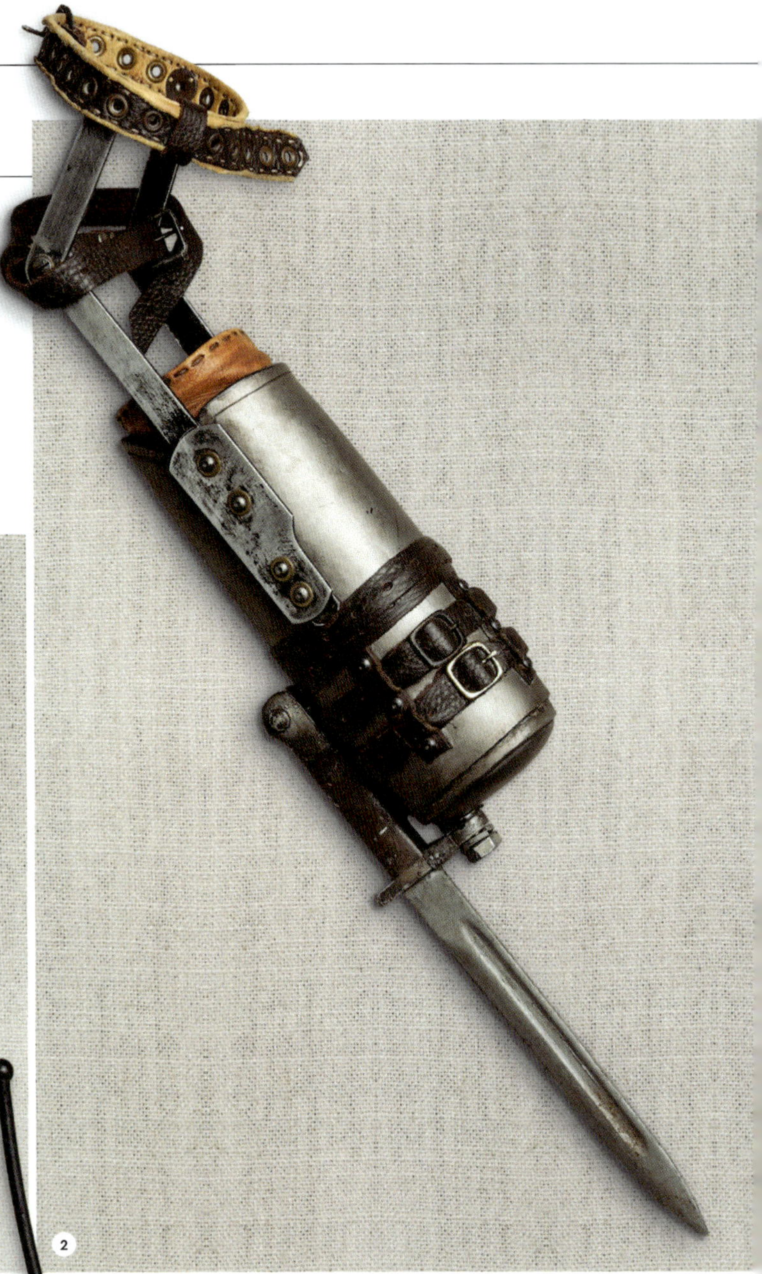

2

6

7

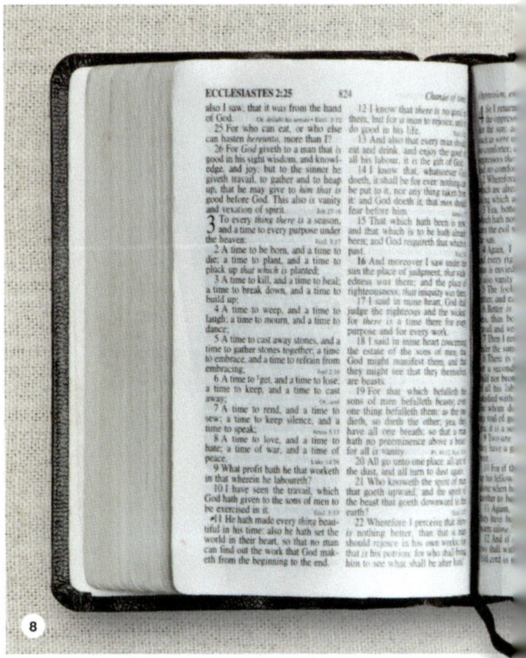

8

PHOTOGRAPHS BY WHITNEY OTT

3

4

5

9

1
SOPHIA'S DOLL
Sanders says the original doll from season 1 had to be replicated twice for use in amped-up stunts (like zombie tramplings). "That doll had its own life," he says.

2
MERLE'S ARM
Left for dead in season 1, Merle reappeared two seasons later—with a badass accessory. "We came up with a Russian bayonet to put on after the arm was built," says prop master John Sanders of the limb developed for Merle by F/X-makeup guru Greg Nicotero. "It turned out to be a great piece."

3
THE SHERIFF HAT
"They don't make it anymore," says costume designer Eulyn C. Womble of Rick's iconic hat, which he later gifted to Carl. "Chandler Riggs's head is growing, so we've had to re-create it. That's been a challenge."

4
DARYL'S NECKLACE
Nicotero made the ears from a mold he had in his shop. The bigger dilemma, says Sanders, was finding "really cool" leather for Daryl to hang them on.

5
MICHONNE'S *KATANA*
Sanders's favorite prop is Michonne's signature weapon, which features an eel-skin grip ("So it won't absorb blood") and a triple goddess symbol that matches the one on his wife's neck. The show uses four identical swords as well as two made of rubber (for rolls or falls) and an aluminum one for "when she hits things."

6
THE GOVERNOR'S EYE PATCH
In a brutal moment in season 3's "Made to Suffer," Michonne stabbed the Governor's right eye with a glass shard. Soon after, he began sporting this stitched leather patch. "The brilliant part is that [David Morrissey] can actually see through it," says Womble. "I thought it was so clever of us."

7
RICK'S RADIO
Season 1 prop master Mike Sabo introduced the walkie-talkie. "Rick gives his last goodbye on that radio," says Sanders. "It had texture and life to it. The dirt and mud say, 'This is the world moving on and on, and everything is getting beat up.'"

8
HERSHEL'S BIBLE
The designers knew Hershel's Bible (which he's carried since season 3) had to be "something not in the ordinary," explains Sanders. "It has a significant look and design—the folded-over locking clasp could fit in your pocket. It was more personal than just a book. It's precious to him."

9
MAGGIE'S WEDDING RINGS
At the end of season 3 Glenn received from Hershel his blessing before proposing to longtime sweetheart Maggie. The story behind the wedding rings was a bit less saccharine: Sanders used an antique set he purchased 20 years ago, which proved "a little tough" to get on (and off) the zombie finger Glenn rips them from.

SEASON 5

The Talk of the Town

The postapocalyptic landscape unearthed a barrage of unique settings in season 5, hopping from creepy man-eating camps and spooky backwoods churches to, finally, a relatively peaceful walled community of survivors called Alexandria

THE NEW SURROUNDINGS WERE A WELCOME dose of variety in a show dominated by forest scenes. "After a while running through the woods does feel a little repetitive," SFX whiz Greg Nicotero conceded at the time.

To the delight of hardcore fans, the season also brought greater fidelity to its source material. "This season is following the comic-book story line pretty closely," Robert Kirkman said at season's onset. "Possibly closer than we ever have before." Showrunner Scott Gimple agreed: "There's just so [many big moments] in the books that I'm excited about getting to."

A barrage of potentially deadly new characters also made their entrances. One important figure to emerge from the comics was Father Gabriel Stokes, the deeply religious minister encountered by the group on the way to Alexandria. Played by

TILL DEATH DO US PART The survivors flee Terminus (left). Comic pages from *The Walking Dead* #69; art by Charlie Adlard and tones by Cliff Rathburn (previous spread).

Seth Gilliam, a standout actor from HBO's *The Wire*, the character's questionable past and traumatized nature added a new sensitivity to Rick's increasingly cold-blooded family group. "Seth is amazing," said Gimple. "He's a tremendous actor."

The Alexandria Safe Zone, also much anticipated from the books, presented a new world for our heroes to navigate. Led by the intelligent and politically calculating Deanna Monroe (Tovah Feldshuh), the villagers didn't uniformly accept their new arrivals, all of whom surrendered their weapons and participated in Deanna's mandatory interviews in order to be welcomed inside the town's walls. "We need people who have lived out there," Deanna tells Rick, asking him to help the sheltered Alexandrians adapt to their new world.

It isn't all that simple. The first encounter with an innocent Alexandrian named Aaron (Ross Marquand) was marked by paranoia and violence, as Aaron was slugged and tied up by Rick, in a stark reminder of how far the group has fallen into darkness since season one. Rick's war-hardened survivors almost entirely regarded the weak, untried Alexandrians as liabilities, which only furthered the division between the two factions.

Tensions increased when Glenn battled a shifty antagonist who was responsible both for the death of newbie Noah (Tyler James Williams) and also blamed Glenn for the death of Deanna's son Aiden (Daniel Bonjour); Carol manipulated the housewives to gain possession of their weapons; and Abraham took command of the construction of a protective wall when the previous crew chief proved inept. But it was Rick's slow-brewing confrontation with the surgeon Pete (Corey Brill), a hard-drinking wife-beater, that left Deanna's husband dead—and gave Rick the opening to seize control of the town.

At season's end the survivors had established a new home in Alexandria, which came complete with its own set of unique vulnerabilities to the outside world. One thing above all was clear: The Ricktatorship was back in effect. Whatever happened from here on out, good or bad, would be on his shoulders. —RAY RAHMAN

▲ **NO ASYLUM** Father Gabriel's church is one of the main locations for the first half of season 5 (top left). Beth and newcomer Noah attempt to escape the Grady Memorial Hospital, wading through a pile of corpses (top right).

◀ **GORE AND MORE** "With my background in premed, I'm all about muscles and ligaments and things," says makeup guru Nicotero, who oversees all of the walkers on the show (far left). Even the confections get the *Walking Dead* makeup treatment. Here, one of the crew eyes a creepy corpse cake (middle). Season 5 introduced some new visual stunts, like this fried zombie (near left).

▲ **REVOLVING DOOR** One man panics; another man dies. Noah (Tyler James Williams) meets a grim end, separated from Glenn by only a pane of glass.

▶ **SIGNS OF LIFE** Rick warns other groups away from Terminus (near right). Extras waiting for their scene attempt to keep cool in Atlanta's heat (middle). Deanna, the conflicted leader of Alexandria, welcomes Rick and the other survivors into her home (far right).

FEAR THE WALKING DEAD

APOCALYPSE SOON

Before the end of the world, there was the beginning of the end of the world. That's where the spin-off *Fear the Walking Dead* starts: a preapocalypse Los Angeles that had only just begun to grapple with the darkness lurking around the corner.

Launched in August 2015 by the same minds behind the flagship series (Robert Kirkman serves as executive producer), the sister series took fans out of the woods and introduced them to a new collection of survivors. *Fear* follows an everyday couple—guidance counselor Madison (Kim Dickens) and teacher Travis (Cliff Curtis)—and their three children. They eventually escape from L.A., trading the city for the sea, and pick up new characters along the way. Over its two seasons, one theme has remained constant: family. "It plays into our biggest fears," said Dickens. "'What if we're not protected? And what if we can't protect ourselves?'" Here are some highlights. —**RAY RAHMAN**

Travis Manawa (Curtis), son Christopher (Lorenzo James Henrie) and Liza (Elizabeth Rodriguez) run for safety in L.A. as panic leads to rioting.

Celia (Marlene Forte) looks after Thomas Abigail (Dougray Scott), whose partner is the mysterious Victor Strand.

A former refugee and a barber by trade, Daniel Salazar (Ruben Blades) trusts few. His daughter Ofelia (Mercedes Mason) does her best to soften his edges.

Victor Strand's (Colman Domingo) plan to escape on his luxury yacht gets derailed quickly—everyone is held hostage by sinister seafarers.

Madison's son Nick (Frank Dillane), a recovering heroin addict with an independent streak, proves to be unusually suited for apocalypse.

Madison (Dickens) goes to great lengths to keep her family, including daughter Alicia (Alycia Debnam-Carey), safe—and together.

MICHAEL CUDLITZ Q&A

Eugene Tells Abraham the Truth

It was the lie that saved two lives. When Abraham (Michael Cudlitz) was at his lowest point and about to commit suicide following the death of his family, a mullet-sporting scientist named Eugene (Josh McDermitt) appeared asking for his help. Eugene's mission—getting to Washington, D.C., to help save mankind—gave Abraham a new purpose for living. It was a win-win situation—that is, until that scientist revealed he had lied in order to secure Abraham's protection. And then, in an instant, all of Abraham's pain returned—right before he delivered some physical pain of his own to Eugene. We spoke to Cudlitz about the takedown. —D.R.

Let's talk about Abraham's reaction to Eugene's big fib that he's not actually a scientist. We get both the calm and then the storm, don't we?
It starts with the repeated failure of Abraham trying to get this mission going and make sure that he gets Eugene to where he needs to get him to. So while Abraham is at his most frayed and very much at the end of his rope, Eugene makes this admission that it's basically all a lie. For Abraham, there's this huge flood. Not only was this all falling apart, he was completely at his wit's end. But then he realizes that every single thing he has done up until this point has basically been for nothing.

But was it more than just the realization of the futility of it all?
It's not only the people that he has killed to keep this guy safe, but it's the people who have died along the way to keep this guy safe. So there's a tremendous amount of turmoil inside of Abraham. He's basically having a nervous breakdown because he can't process all of this at once. And then for some reason, Eugene thinks it would be wise to point out that he is actually smarter than Abraham.

And that's the snapping point? Because up until then, it looks like Abraham's mind is in another place.
He's trying to process everything that's gone on. It's like, "What? Are you f---ing kidding me?" He realizes that this is the truth. He's just putting everything together in his head until he says that one specific piece of dialogue, and then everything turns to anger and gets unleashed on Eugene.

How do you transition from such a quiet place to immediate pure and utter rage?
I think it's simmering. You push it down. The strength of the show is that the circumstances and the reality are so heightened, but it has to be grounded in a very real place or else it doesn't work. Because we have so many "ridiculous" things that we do, if it's not anchored in reality, I don't think it's believable at all.

So you pop Josh a bunch of times in the face in front of that fire truck. I know precautions are being taken, but how do you sell that aggression while making sure you don't actually hurt your fellow actor?
Things are planned out very specifically, and cameras are placed in the exact proper place. That particular fight sequence—or ass-whooping sequence, I guess you'd call it, because it's more of a beating that is handed out—was shot in such a way that it was very easy to keep everyone safe. I was very far away from Josh at all times. They shot it with a long lens, which compresses all the action. As long as I'm in between him [and the camera] and he's reacting properly, it sells.

Do accidents ever happen?
Sure. I've been punched square in the face many a time. Never on this show, but it happens. We try not to do it, but everybody understands that there's a little bit of a risk involved. Nobody's going to die, you know?

What's so fascinating about this scene is that while Eugene lied to Abraham to save himself, he really saved Abraham with that lie as well.
Absolutely. He saved his life, and that's not lost on Abraham over the course of the series, and that is why there is such an affinity. You can go back even to when they hadn't made up yet, when Eugene goes to drink the water that was left by Aaron on the road, and Abraham smacks it out of his hand, because protecting him is so ingrained in him. And he's not sure anymore at that point if it's just a habit or if he actually has genuine feelings for this person. And as we realize through the series and up until last season's finale, he absolutely does.

DARK TIMES AHEAD Immediately after the big reveal, McDermitt got a shaky reception from fans of the show. "Eugene isn't everyone's favorite person at that point," McDermitt says with a sigh. "I literally [had] people screaming 'Liar!' at me on the street. But I would rather have them screaming that than 'Pervert!'" With the revelation of Eugene's deception, on top of the killing of Beth at the hospital, it's fair to say the group had seen better days. "They're lost emotionally and geographically," says Scott Gimple. "They don't know which direction is safety, they don't know which direction is hope, and things are going to get worse before they get better."

You Can Live in Alexandria

The sleepy town where the series films is an actual Georgia development. Its residents try to carry on as normal despite the influx of zombies. Call it the cost of living—with the undead. —DALTON ROSS

YES, PEOPLE ACTUALLY LIVE HERE. During the filming of the big fight scene between Rick and Pete near the end of season 5, the take was momentarily halted while a mail truck drove through to deliver catalogs and bills to residents of the community.

Fictional Alexandria is also literally right on the other side of the train tracks from another iconic *Walking Dead* setting: Woodbury. That's right, you can see one town from the other. In fact, while filming in Alexandria, *Walking Dead* cast members would often walk over to Woodbury for a coffee pick-me-up.

The Gin Property development was built by Scott Tigchelaar, the president of Raleigh Studios Atlanta, the home base for *The Walking Dead* in Senoia. (The famous prison from seasons 3 and 4 was built onto the back of Raleigh.) And as *Walking Dead* exec producer Gale Anne Hurd explains, Gin Property was specifically built to also be used as a live set.

"Luckily the community was developed by the same people who own the studios," Hurd tells *EW*. "Part of the covenant in the CC&Rs of that community is that it is designed to be a haven and a draw for filming, so that's something that all the residents there were aware of—[though initially they] may have forgotten. But I have a feeling the blasting lights at 3 in the morning probably reminded them."

CC&Rs stands for Covenants, Conditions & Restrictions, which basically are rules placed on homes by—in this case—a developer. So if you want to buy a house and live there, you agree to the conditions. And now one of those conditions has become a giant 15-ft. wall around the majority of the property to simulate the wall keeping the zombies away from Alexandria. According to the *Newnan Times-Herald*, the studio had even obtained a permit for the wall. That's a lot of wall. Alexandria remains an active community in the comic books, so they could be there for a while.

Kathleen Sullivan, who lives on Plyant Street in the community, did not sound particularly enthused about the enclosure when she spoke to the *Times-Herald*. "I said that the wall would be ugly. None of us had seen it yet. But OMG, it is uglier than I could ever imagine."

While residents have to worry about a big wall surrounding their houses for a while longer, the show has to worry about spoilers from nosy neighbors who may want to leak details of what they see or sneakily take unauthorized images. However, Hurd says that's actually less of an issue than when they film in other locations. "The truth is, we face it wherever we go when we're outside the studio property," says Hurd. "At least there isn't a home that is six stories high where they can actually get a lens focused on us. The area that we film in primarily, the houses are empty. The people have decided while we're there to live elsewhere—or they understand and respect the rules."

In the end it sounds like the local homeowners and *The Walking Dead*'s crew have learned to coexist and deal with the inconveniences on both sides. "I think the biggest issue is really access," Hurd says. "People want to be able to get home when they drive up, and that isn't always the case because we're in the middle of a shot. But we try to be respectful to that part of the neighborhood and understand that these are people's lives. We're there, they're there."

That integration has led to a few awkward moments. "We're shooting scenes in this [supposedly deserted] town and you see the curtains move in somebody's window, and there are people living in there!" says cast member Melissa McBride. "And you look over and they wave, and then the mail truck comes through."

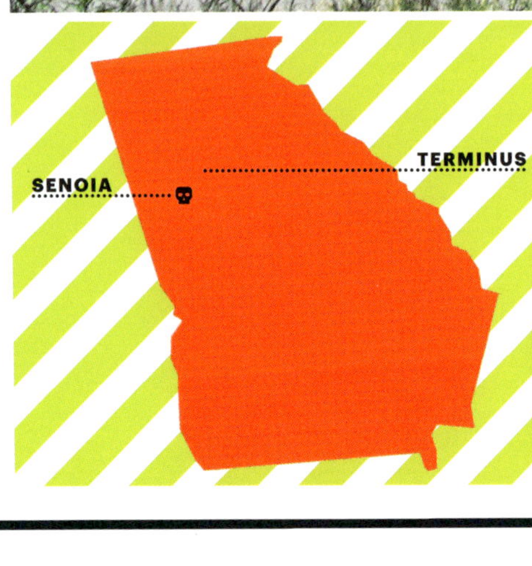

NEIGHBORHOOD WATCH Top: Rick and Carl eyeball their new home with Aaron (Ross Marquand). Bottom: a map of the real location of Senoia, geographically much closer to Terminus than Virginia (far left), the literal writing on the wall (center); and the gutted interior of a Gin Properties facade (left).

Inside the Mind of Robert Kirkman

The man behind the *Walking Dead* comic book was as surprised as anyone that his tale about a sheriff's deputy fighting zombies would conquer TV and become a global phenomenon. Here he talks about the triumphs, the failures and the end he has planned for the graphic novel that started it all. —DALTON ROSS

If you had to choose one, which is your favorite issue of the comic?

My mindset is that I don't like any of them, and every month I'm trying to do a good one. That's the kind of thing that keeps me going, like, "I'm going to try harder and make this one better." So I like to think that every issue is better than the last, but I know that's not the case. I guess if I had to pick one favorite moment in the story, it's probably issue 50 where Carl and Rick are alone after the prison attack, and Rick is seemingly dying, and it's just an entire issue of Carl trying to survive on his own and thinking he can't until realizing that he really can. That was a fun story and a big turning point for Carl—and I actually got to write that episode of the show, so that was a lot of fun too.

You've mentioned before that you wish you hadn't gone and chopped Rick's hand off, because that now poses logistical issue that always need to be considered. What else in the comics do you wish you could take back or change?

There are constantly things in the show where I'm like, "You know, the show's Carol is so much better than the comic book Carol." I like the comic book Carol—there are definitely some cool stories that were done with her—but it didn't do anything as cool as what we do in the show with her. So there are things like that, where if I look at the show and I look at the comic, it's like I kind of wish I had done something like that in the comic.

Besides Rick Grimes, who is your favorite comic book character?

You know, I don't really have a favorite. I tend to kill those, just because when I find myself really attached to a character, or if I find myself wanting to write them more and more and steering more story toward them, I kind of realize that that means the audience investment in that character is extremely high, and I don't want it to affect the story too much by focusing too much on that character. And that tends to make me want to kill them.

When you are doing something big in the comic book, like killing a main character, do you communicate that to the showrunner, Scott Gimple, and AMC in advance?

No, there's no communication whatsoever. They have no approval over what happens in the comic. Scott Gimple is an avid reader of the comic and prefers to experience the comic book as a reader, so he gets the advance issues as they're published, but he doesn't read scripts. He gets mad at me if I give him any kind of indication as to what's coming, because he doesn't like spoilers. So they're kind of 100 percent in the dark, which I guess is pretty remarkable, and I would probably say it's a testament to the trust that AMC has in me. I mean, I guess to a certain extent at this point the comic book is kind of a workshop of future seasons of the show, and it's fun to think that I can just completely torpedo the story if I wanted to.

You have an endpoint in mind in terms of how the story finishes, right?

Yeah, I know exactly how it ends, and I'm always taking baby steps toward that point as I'm telling the story. I know what the end point is, and at the end of the day, I want this entire long narrative to be a complete story with a beginning, middle and end. We're just spending a lot of time in the middle, so I kind of have to know what that direction is, and I have to know what that end point is to be able to keep building toward it. I think that's the only way to keep it alive.

"I DON'T REALLY HAVE A FAVORITE [CHARACTER]. I TEND TO KILL THOSE"

—ROBERT KIRKMAN

GRAPHIC CONTENT Above: Kirkman in Los Angeles. Below, from left to right: *The Walking Dead* No. 1, originally published Oct. 8, 2003, drawn by Tony Moore; No. 66, from October 2009, drawn by Charlie Adlard and Cliff Rathburn; and No. 158, the Sept. 7, 2016, issue, drawn by Adlard, Stefano Gaudiano and Rathburn.

SEASON 6

Shock & Awesome

For years *The Walking Dead* was controversial for its cringe-inducing imagery. In season 6 it gained notoriety for what it *didn't* show. Fans were left in the dark as the cliff-hangers just kept coming

WHILE WRITERS LEFT QUESTIONS UNANSWERED, the series satisfied in other ways, including ramping up the sheer number of zombies threatening the survivors and their new stronghold in Alexandria. One filming day for the season premiere alone featured 300 flesh eaters, a full hundred more than the show's previous high. "This season we've sort of played up the idea that skin is no longer able to maintain any adhesion to the muscle so it just starts sloughing off," explains makeup guru Greg Nicotero, who intentionally altered the appearance of the walkers to reflect the decomposition that comes with time.

The show also welcomed a key original back to the fold: Rick's old pacifist frenemy Morgan Jones. Like others before him, Morgan forced the group to think about what they were doing and why they were doing it—a point given extra heft by Lennie James's memorable performance.

HOGGING THE ROAD Daryl draws the attention of a walker horde (left). Comic pages from *The Walking Dead* #84; art by Charlie Adlard and tones by Cliff Rathburn (previous spread).

"Having Lennie—who was such a huge part of season 1 and amazing every time we had him back—finally be a regular part of this show is really going to energize it," Robert Kirkman says. Norman Reedus expressed similar feelings: "I remember seeing Lennie in the opening episode on the first season, and I was like, 'Who is that guy? He's great!' Everyone had talked about working with him and how awesome he is."

But all is not as rosy as it seems. James points out that the Morgan/Rick relationship is quite complicated. "That people see them as old friends is not entirely true to the facts," says James. "The first time the two of them met, Morgan stuck a gun in Rick's face. The second time they met, Morgan tried to kill Rick."

Another character who didn't prompt such a warm initial reaction was Negan (played by Jeffrey Dean Morgan). Foul-mouthed and leather-clad, sporting a baseball bat wrapped in barbed wire (and named Lucille!) plus a mean mustache, one of the comic book's biggest baddies inspired fear the moment he walked onto the set. "He's just kind of a charismatic leader," Morgan says of his villain. "People are probably a little scared of him. But in this *Walking Dead* world, people are going to follow a guy like that. Just like Rick.... They're just two sides of the same coin, really." Kirkman is less subtle. "Negan is kind of an atomic bomb," he says.

And the explosion came at the very end of the season, with a finale that found Negan swinging his bat and killing one of our heroes. The problem? We don't know which one—it was yet another cliff-hanger that left viewers twisting in the wind. Kirkman offered only the slightest of hints at the time, saying, "The show will probably never be the same after that."

Fan reaction to the season's ending was mixed, ranging from confusion to outrage. Showrunner Scott Gimple and Kirkman have both stated they know that by making fans wait for the payoff, they have to earn it with a satisfactory conclusion. Reedus promises that they will. "I think probably the planet is going to explode. That's my feeling," he adds, "It's worth the wait, trust me." —RAY RAHMAN

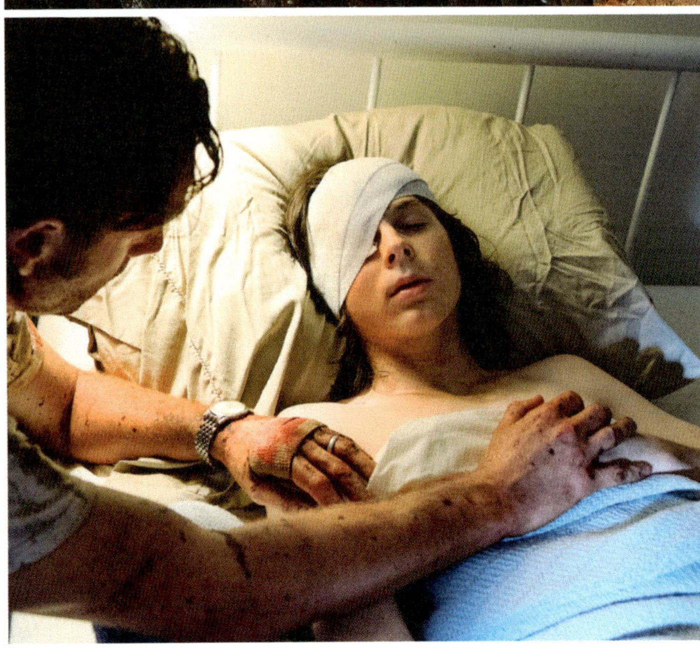

▲

RISKY BUSINESS Paul "Jesus" Rovia (Tom Payne) welcomes several members of Rick's group into the Hilltop, a prelude to proposing an alliance against the Saviors (left). Rick considers the coalition (right).

◀

EYE ON THE PRIZE Carl recovers after receiving a stray bullet to the face (left). Greg Nicotero as a walker, planning the next scene (middle). Carol, disguised as a Wolf, sneaks Morgan back to freedom (right).

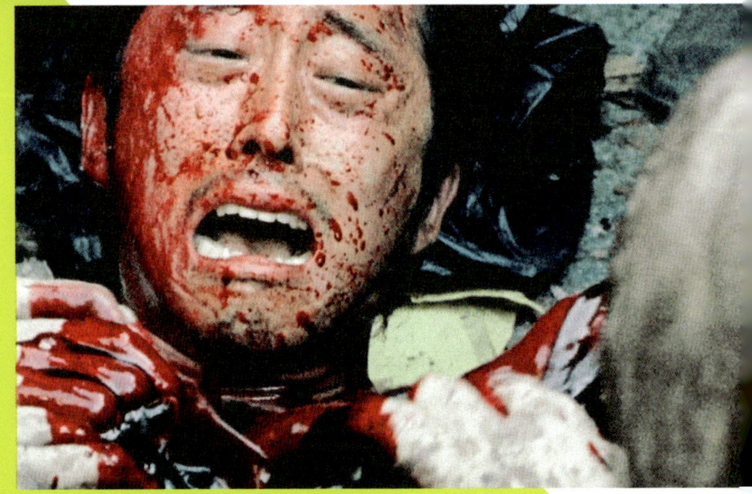

LAST MAN STANDING Negan introduces Rick's group to his baseball bat, Lucille, in the polarizing cliff-hanger.

INTO THE GREAT UNKNOWN Glenn's fate was in limbo for a big part of the season—intentionally. Kirkman says the goal was to "put our audiences in the exact same position that Maggie was in" by not knowing if he lived or died (left). Maggie, with Xander Berkeley as Gregory, the leader of the Hilltop Colony (right).

DYNAMIC DUOS

LOVE IN THE TIME OF THE WALKERS

Survivors, warriors, killers…lovers? Romance found ways to flourish despite all odds. Whether it's a dramatic three-character tango (hey there, Shane) or something more understated (we see you, Noah and Beth), the series has made a point of proving time and again that as long as people survive, so too will love. These characters had the heart (and guts) to find their soulmates—and got us rooting for their relationships. —**RAY RAHMAN**

GLENN AND MAGGIE
Their story seems downright traditional (albeit with more zombies). How many couples on the show have actually gotten married, and with the father of the bride's approval, no less? "Your world is who you're with," Steven Yeun says of Glenn and Maggie's bond. "The world is the people that you love.…If it's not with them, then what's the point of continuing on?"

ABRAHAM AND ROSITA
Love can be fleeting. Abraham and Rosita fell for each other, and they quickly became a hot-and-heavy couple (just ask Eugene). Their messy breakup a season later, when Abraham became interested in Sasha, broke Rosita's heart. "When I first met you, I thought you were the last woman on earth," he told Rosita. "You're not."

RICK AND MICHONNE
They always made for logical partners: two leaders, both protective and fiercely loyal. They even formed a makeshift family unit—which made the "Richonne" moment so natural. "These are two people who have suddenly realized…what they already had together and who they already were to each other," Scott Gimple says. "This isn't a one-night stand."

DARYL AND CAROL
The most enduring types of love are often left unspoken. That's especially true when it comes to Daryl, who never has been much for words. While Daryl and Carol's will-they/won't-they relationship has kept viewers hooked, Norman Reedus is playing the long game. "I want her to make the first move," he says. "I want it to be awkward when it happens."

DANAI GURIRA Q&A

Michonne & Carl (& Rick) Bond

Actress Danai Gurira details the emotional scene that allowed her warrior character to let down her guard and listen to her heart. Sometimes a small, quiet scene can be as important as a big, emotional one. Take the moment between Michonne (Danai Gurira) and Carl (Chandler Riggs) that takes place on the porch in the episode "The Next World." Earlier, Michonne watched Carl out in the woods as he risked his life to herd the zombie Deanna so her son Spencer could put her to rest. When she confronted Carl about it while he was getting ready to put baby Judith to bed, what followed was a tender exchange that demonstrated Michonne's return as a maternal figure, which led directly to the romantic encounter with Rick. —D. R.

What are some of your recollections of this pivotal scene?

Michonne has so much respect for this child soldier who's weathered so much. That's so much a part of why she loves him and wants to protect him. Her approach, I felt, needed to be gentle and respectful but also clear and firm, that they are going to have this conversation. And he is, of course, avoiding that. It was interesting to find the moments where he has to finally open up about what exactly he was doing out there, and that takes her by great surprise.

And this changes Michonne?

It's a really beautiful part of her evolution—the realization that he looks at her with that level of regard and that she is actually that loved by him. She comes back to this young man whom she just absolutely loved and hears him affirm that fact by leaving her the position of mother in his heart. That really makes her so emotionally open and available. It was really a climactic moment because it causes her to have an open enough heart and available enough emotional space to have that next moment with his father.

Everyone talks about the Rick and Michonne connection now for pretty obvious reasons, but the Michonne and Carl connection has always been just as significant, albeit in a different way.

Carl's the one who actually brought her into the group. From there on out, they definitely had a deep and intimate bond. The loss of a child, many will say, is the worst loss one can have, and Carl steps into that position of giving her a second experience with a young, growing man that she lost with her own son. So he opens the gates of her heart to be able to open up to Rick.

I don't know if she would've been able to respond to Rick's touch in that next scene [otherwise], honestly. I think she would've felt that electricity between her and him, but she probably would have said, "Okay, don't stay up too late," and said something cocky and jumped off to bed. But I think that what happened with Carl opens up her heart to give and receive the love. She's like, This is my family.

Do you think it was as if Carl was almost giving her permission to let that moment with Rick happen?

Absolutely. He blesses her with this position in their home, and I think it gives her permission to be open, to let go a little bit and to let her heart actually express itself. The idea of having her heart touched so unexpectedly by Carl in that previous scene, it allows her heart to take the driver's seat.

Looking at Michonne's journey since we first met her, how has she changed?

She was covered in armor that was impenetrable, and piece by piece, season by season,

the armor's been removed. But it hasn't made her weak—it's just made her strong in a different way. That warrior hasn't gone away, but she started to find her voice and open up.

Finally, I have to know: How much did the baby playing Judith cooperate in this scene?
She was amazing! Every single take of the scene with me hugging Chandler while he held her in his arms, when I would break away from him [after we stopped rolling] she would look up at me and reach out her arms for me to take her so she could hug me. Every single take. And I would have to take her and hug her. It was incredibly adorable.

A PAIR OF ACES In the comics Rick begins a relationship with Andrea around this time, but as she perished in season 3, that wasn't a valid option. Scott Gimple explains that the Andrea storyline has been divided up between several other characters, but the Michonne/Rick pairing just made sense. "These are two people who have found kindred spirits in each other—[they value] strength, respect, support, loyalty," he says. "But the world has been screaming in their faces and clawing at them for a good part of their acquaintance. For all they've been through, when the world stopped screaming and clawing for them, they realized what they had."

The Dearly Departed

The only thing more lethal than a horde of walkers is *TWD's* bloodthirsty writing team. We caught up with former cast members to find out how they felt when they heard they were getting bitten out of the show. —DALTON ROSS

1

TYREESE *Chad L. Coleman*

HOW HE DIED ***Chomped by Noah's zombified brother at the Shirewilt Estates in season 5***

Viewers weren't the only ones surprised by Tyreese's demise. "I was shocked," says Coleman about finding out his fate. "They caught me off guard. I didn't see it coming." Coleman hopes that fans recall him as the gentle giant who refused to give in to the violence of the world around him: "Remember his humanity and kindness and generosity of spirit. I know it touched people, and hopefully we can be in touch with that part of ourselves—what I consider to be the better part of ourselves." And yes, the actor (who currently stars on Syfy's *The Expanse*) still keeps up with the show. "I'm curious about my sister and Abraham," Coleman says. "What is that about? I guess that's being a brother. I don't see it."

2

SAM *Robin Lord Taylor*

HOW HE DIED ***Had his throat slit at the Terminus trough in the season 5 premiere***

Even though Taylor landed the coveted role of the Penguin on *Gotham* after his brief season 4 appearance, he made it a point to return for his big death cameo. "I was so happy to have my own closure and see everybody one last time," says Taylor. "The *Walking Dead* family, it's a real thing. I'm so honored to be a part of it."

3

SOPHIA *Madison Lintz*

HOW SHE DIED ***Went missing in the season 2 premiere, only to be found as a zombie walking out of Hershel's barn in the midseason finale, where she was mercy-killed by Rick***

Lintz was only 12 when she shot her harrowing death scene, but even though the now 17-year-old was at the center of one of *The Walking Dead*'s most memorable moments ever, she no longer watches the show. "I think I stopped watching at around season 3," she says. "Just because it's a little bit gory for me. It's so weird, because when I was younger, I was like, 'This is the coolest thing ever!'"

4

NOAH *Tyler James Williams*

HOW HE DIED ***Devoured in a revolving door in season 5 after Nicholas left him and Glenn to die***

Williams was of two minds when he first learned about Noah's death—upset to leave the show yet appreciative of the way his demise would propel Glenn's story forward. "Having been him, I love him," Williams told *EW* last year. "I really want the best for him. But as a fan of the show, I was like, 'You've got to go.' He's an omen, essentially. He's got to die. But one of the things that's really interesting—having gone through the death and all that—is that it allows me to be a fan of the show again." File that one under "Silver Linings."

5

LIZZIE *Brighton Sharbino*

HOW SHE DIED ***After killing sister Mika in season 4, Lizzie was told to "look at the flowers" while Carol put a bullet in her brain***

There is one thing Sharbino will not miss about her time on *The Walking Dead*. "They would put a bunch of dirt on you," she says. "Sometimes I would forget to take off the makeup when I left set, and everyone would just be staring at me like, 'Is this girl okay?'" Due to her somewhat deranged character (who befriended zombies and thought she could kill people without harming them), Sharbino gets somewhat deranged requests. "People will come up and have me pretend to suffocate their baby for a picture," she says. "And someone licked my hand. No one prepares you for what to do when someone licks your hand."

PHOTOGRAPHS BY ETHAN HILL

6 JACQUI *Jeryl Prescott*

HOW SHE DIED ***Committed suicide by allowing herself to be blown up at the CDC in the season 1 finale***

Prescott says Jacqui's fate kept changing right up to the filming of the season 1 finale because original showrunner Frank Darabont "was going back and forth about whether or not he wanted Jacqui to die. There were three possibilities as I recall: that Jacqui would not die; that Jacqui would die, but she would die at the top of season 2; or that Jacqui would just die in the explosion at the end of season 1." While Darabont ultimately went with option No. 3, Prescott notes that "it's nice to be the only one to go in such a flame of glory."

7 THE GOVERNOR *David Morrissey*

HOW HE DIED ***Stabbed by Michonne and then shot by girlfriend Lilly in season 4 while attempting to take over the prison***

"It takes a lot of people to kill the Governor," jokes Morrissey about the one-two punch of Michonne and Lilly that took him down. The only regret about his character's final chapter? "I was sad to have to kill Scott Wilson as Hershel, because he's a great friend of mine." In fact, the actors formed their own two-man support group. "When it was my last day, Scott came back and watched me go, and then he and I went out for a drink and had a meal."

8 MIKA *Kyla Kenedy*

HOW SHE DIED ***Sister Lizzie knifed her in season 4, mistakenly believing Mika would come back to life. Whoops!***

"It was a very intense scene," says Kenedy in perhaps the understatement of the century. The end was an emotional one offscreen as well. "It was so sad. I didn't want to leave everyone on-set because it was such a great environment."

9 BOB *Lawrence Gilliard Jr.*

HOW HE DIED ***Was bitten by a zombie and then captured and partially eaten by the Terminus group in season 5***

Gilliard had strong thoughts about characters being killed off even before he appeared on the show, thanks to his early expiration on *The Wire*. "I really don't dig that part of TV nowadays," he told *EW* after being cast as Bob in 2013. "Personally, I think this is unfair to the actors because we've got families, and we should know if we're going to have a job next week. I don't watch a lot of TV today because I don't like becoming attached to characters and watching them get killed off."

10 BETH *Emily Kinney*

HOW SHE DIED ***Accidentally shot by Officer Dawn Lerner in season 5 after Beth impaled her with a pair of scissors at the hospital***

The Walking Dead is notorious for building characters up only to tear them down, and Beth Greene is a prime example. "It was shocking to both me and the audience, because we were both just getting to see more of Beth and understanding her point of view," says Kinney. "In some ways, we were just seeing the beginnings of the character, which made her death especially sad." But Beth isn't totally dead to the actress. "People call me Beth all the time," she says.

11 T-DOG *IronE Singleton*

HOW HE DIED ***Eaten by zombies in the prison in season 3 while helping Carol escape***

Rather than mourn his death, Singleton celebrates the fact that T-Dog lasted as long as he did. "I was told that I would only do two episodes, so I wasn't shocked when I got the call," he says. "T-Dog's probably the only one who has died heroically. You can't find a better way to die than that."

SPECIAL THANKS
Brad Beatson, Nicole Fisher, Kristina Jutzi, Seniqua Koger, Christine Ramage, Kate Roncinske

Published by Time Inc. Books
225 Liberty Street
New York, NY 10281

We welcome your comments and suggestions about Entertainment Weekly Books. Please write to us at: Entertainment Weekly Books, Attention: Book Editors, P.O. Box 62310, Tampa, FL 33662-2310
If you would like to order any of our hardcover Collector's Edition books, please call us at 800-327-6388, Monday through Friday, 7 a.m.–9 p.m. Central Time.

PHOTO CREDITS
COVER #1 (clockwise) Zombie/Walker photographed by Dan Winters; Reedus, Lincoln: Frank Ockenfels 3/AMC (2); Yeun, Gurira, Cudlitz: Gene Page/AMC (3); **COVER #2** Yuen, Cudlitz, McBride, Riggs. Martin-Green, James: Gene Page/AMC (6); Kinney, Cohan, Coleman, Lincoln, WIlson: Frank Ockenfels 3/AMC (5); Reedus, Gurira: Photographed by Photograph by Frank Ockenfels 3 (2); **BACK COVER** Behind the Scenes:Gene Page/AMC; **Pg 4-5:** *Talking Dead*: Jordin Althaus/AMC (2); Hardwick, Lincoln, Yeun: Kevin Winter/Getty Images; Hardwick: Jason Kempin/Getty Images; **Pg 6-7:** (clockwise) *World War Z*: Jaap Buitendijk; *Teenage Zombies*: Everett Collection; *Night of the Living Dead*: Image Ten/Photofest; **Pg 8-9:** (clockwise) *28 Days Later...*: Peter Mountain; *Resident Evil*: Courtesy Capcom; *Dawn of the Dead*: United/Everett Collection; *iZombie*: Cate Cameron/The CW; *Shaun of the Dead*: Rogue Pictures/Everett Collection; **Pg 12-14:** Gene Page/AMC (6); **Pg 15:** Charlie Adlard/Skybound/Image Comics (2); **Pg. 16-17:** Tony Moore (2); **Pg 18-23:** Scott Garfield/AMC (9); Gene Page/AMC (5) **Pg 24-25:** Scott Garfield/AMC (2); Instagram pics: Courtesy Jaime Miller (5); **Pg 28-29:** *Love Actually*: Peter Mountain; *Lucky Break*: Film Four/Fragile Films/Kobal Collection; **Pg 30-31:** *Mercy*: Universal/Photofest; *The Boondock Saints*: Franchise Pictures/Brood Syndicate/Kobal Collection; **Pg 32-33:** Charlie Adlard (2); **Pg 34-35:** Gene Page/AMC; **Pg 36-37:** *The Walking Dead* (group): Bob Mahoney/AMC; *The Walking Dead*: Gene Page/AMC (4); **Pg 38-39:** *The Walking Dead* (group): Russell Kaye/AMC; Bernthal, Lincoln: Gene Page/AMC (2); Yeun and Cohan: Bob Mahoney/AMC; **Pg 39:** (from top): Scott Garfield/AMC (2); Gene Page/AMC; Russell Kaye/AMC; **Pg 40-41:** Lintz, Gimple: Gene Page/AMC (2); **Pg 42-43:** AMC; **Pg 44-45:** Charlie Adlard; **Pg 46-47:** Blake Tyers/AMC; **Pg 48-49:** (clockwise) *The Walking Dead*: Gene Page/AMC (4); Morrissey and Szymanski: Russell Kaye/AMC; **Pg 50-51:** (clockwise) Reedus and Rooker: Tina Rowden/AMC; *The Walking Dead*: Gene Page/AMC (4); **Pg 51:** Gene Page/AMC (4); **Pg 54-57:** Steven Yeun (8); **Pg 58-59:** Charlie Adlard; **Pg 60-64:** Gene Page/AMC (9); **Pg 65:** *The Walking Dead*: Gene Page/AMC (4); CDC: Scott Garfield/AMC; **Pg 66-67:** Gene Page/AMC (4); **Pg 70-71:** Charlie Adlard; **Pg 72-76:** Gene Page/AMC (10); **Pg 77:** (from top): Curtis, Rodriguez, Henrie: Justina Mintz/AMC; *Fear the Walking Dead*: Richard Foreman Jr/AMC (5); **Pg 78-79:** Gene Page/AMC; **Pg 80-81:** *The Walking Dead*: Gene Page/AMC (2); Georgia map: Chokkicx/Getty Images; Burned home: AMC; **Pg 82-83:** Kirkman: Christopher Patey/Contour by Getty Images; Comic covers: Courtesy Skybound (3); **Pg 84-85:** Charlie Adlard; **Pg 86-90:** Gene Page/AMC (8); **Pg 91:** Gene Page/AMC (4); **Pg 92-93:** Gene Page/AMC (2)

PHOTOGRAPH BY DYLAN COULTER

19550811R00055

Printed in Great Britain
by Amazon